Patchwork

Jan Harwood

ISBN: 979-8-218-35270-7

Dedicated to my grandchildren, Griffin, Emaline, and Juliet, with hope that these true stories of my life might help you to know and love your dear selves better...

And to my dear friends, the poet and humanitarian, Ruth Gunn Mota, who read these tales with lots of laughs and shrewd perception; and my unquenchable college roomy, Bertha Blattner, who has stuck around through thick and thin, cheering me with her matchless dry wit. I can't sufficiently express my gratitude to my women's group—Karen, Ellen, Lisa—which has become a true sisterhood in fifty years of sharing our lives in the way that only women can do.

Contents

Introduction

I've always saved scraps of cotton and velvet from my old shirts and dresses that were too worn out for Goodwill, hoping that someday I'd have time, leisure and energy to make a patchwork quilt. To my joy, such a blessed time actually came: soon after I retired and settled into my pink Spanish-style cottage in weird, wonderful Santa Cruz, and realized that I could finally rid my closet of those bulky boxes of swatches!

My Granny had sewed many lovely quilts, including one she made especially for me—a pattern of multicolored hexagonal flowers on a white background with a border of bright red triangles. I dearly cherished it, but in my carelessness, I wore it out by using it on my bed all the time and letting my toddlers romp on it, so that it required frequent laundering, and finally expired in rags.

I knew very little about the mechanics of quilting, so I got books from the library, bought a secondhand wooden stretcher and packets of heavy, strangely shaped needles and lots of red thread. I chose a traditional Log Cabin pattern (because of its beauty and simplicity, and because it reminds me of my favorite president).

I went right at it, and now for some twenty years, my bright, imperfect, but lovingly crafted quilt, made entirely by hand, has brightened and warmed my bed, while reminding me that I am capable of careful, considered workmanship when I really try.

Nowadays, like many who've been lucky enough to live to a ripe, meaning really, really old age, I sometimes discover—wrapped in dusty burlap and buried deep in the jumbled warehouse of my brain—vivid images of dramatic or joyous or painful events from my life which have special meaning to me. And then I write the stories.

I've written many stories, first in my head and then in a splendid class, aptly called "Writing About Our Lives," led by the marvelous poet, Ellen Bass.

This book, then, is a crazy-quilt of my life, in no particular pattern—haphazard, colorful, true, and carefully wrought. I hope you have the good luck to piece your own quilt, someday.

I've used real names for myself and my family, and pseudonyms for anyone who wouldn't like to be identified.

WHEN I'M GONE

When I'm gone, you know
I won't be, really.
All the stuff I've accumulated,
cherished or hated,
beloved others will have to deal with then
and when that's done
for a few generations there'll be memories,
pictures, songs and stories
tinged with my peculiar take,
and remnants of many pies I stuck my finger in whether it was
wanted or not.
Most of all, I expect,
you'll find my powerful love;
it's lodged in nooks and crannies all over the place,
and you'll never entirely get rid of it.

Clockwise from top left: Baby Jan; High School Senior, age 17; grown-up Jan (in Italian hat); age 5 with brother Garth, age 2. Old Jan: *see back cover*

A Family Love Story
For our children

East Tenth Street

It was Thanksgiving Eve, 1954. I'd graduated from Missouri University in June, and as soon as I earned enough money (I figured a hundred dollars would get me started), I left Kansas City forever, on a Greyhound to Manhattan. To my astonishment, my parents, still in their mid-forties, and my younger brother, Garth, with his new wife, Ruthie, would soon shift the whole clan—minus me—to Miami, Florida: I guess we were all looking for dramatic changes in our lives. Since then, I had lived a lonely, but ecstatically expectant life in a rented room in a building on the corner of 113th Street and Broadway, near Columbia University.

My tedious job as a clerical assistant in a doctor's office at Bellevue Hospital wasn't quite what I'd hoped for when I left Kansas City with my shiny new MA in Philosophy, but my life was crammed with joyful exploration and small adventures. I was twenty-three, free at last from my family and the Midwest —and I was in New York City, where everything is! I had evenings and weekends to explore a cosmopolitan world of multiethnic neighborhoods, shops, galleries and museums, the ballet, concerts, street markets, parks, and the subway—in those days, such places were relatively safe for a young woman alone.

As a girl of the 50's, of course, I lived constantly in hope of a great romance, which, I felt, was all but guaranteed to materialize in this melting pot of the best and brightest. But in fact, I'd made only a couple of new friends, and no fascinating lovers had yet appeared at any of the venues I hopefully explored. (It simply never occurred to me to enter a bar alone, which might have attracted more male attention, but that was outside my known universe of romantic possibilities.)

As the holidays approached—the first ever that I would spend away from home—I decided to drop in on a young woman, Rose Milton, who had been in some of my classes at M.U. A mutual friend had written me, mentioned that Rose was also in the city, and suggested I look her up. I had the address, not far from Bellevue—but no phone number. So, after work that Thanksgiving eve, I took the subway down to Third Avenue at Tenth Street—the heart of the infamous Bowery, where drunks and other homeless folks hung out under the El— the elevated railroad—which created a long, shadowy zone where seedy people congregated, and low taverns, pawn shops and flophouses accumulated.

I picked my way across the littered street, stepping carefully around a man passed out cold—or dead?—with a bottle in one outstretched hand—and went up the filthy steps of a narrow three-story brick building, at 89 E. Tenth. It was identical to several other adjoined buildings, except that on the sidewalk level, there was a grimy drinking establishment with partially burned-out neon beer signs, and on the floor above it, long windows curtained with black sheets. There were no doorbells or slots with tenants' names, so I opened the battered front door and climbed the dimly lit steps inside with increasing doubt about the wisdom of this holiday visit. How in the world could Rose Milton, the refined young woman, whose allure to men I had envied at the university, possibly live here, in these deplorable conditions? The stairwell reeked of urine and stale alcohol.

No one to ask, so I knocked at the first door I came to. It was newly painted, shiny black, but pitted and gouged, layered with generations of un-sanded paint jobs.

The door opened promptly—but what confronted me was clearly not my old schoolmate. Instead, I saw a huge, bright smile on a handsome young male face, obviously delighted to see me—so reassuring in the scary, dingy darkness of that melancholy building. Although this (for all I knew) possibly rapacious, maniacal killer stood there, wearing only old black swim trunks, with a large mallet in one hand, I, like the dopey Missouri hick that I was, trusted him at once. I entered the door at his unrefusable invitation.

"Rose? Sure, she lives here, but she's not home yet—you want to come in and wait for her?"

Broad, sunny grin, shock of shaggy blond hair, curly golden mat on his bare chest; slender build, muscular arms—baby-blue eyes. My type, exactly (though I hadn't known this before). But, I reflected, he was obviously living with Rose, the femme fatale of the M.U. Philosophy Department, who was graced with a small, delicately sculptured nose and aquamarine eyes.

"Have a seat!" He looked around for the one paint-spattered wooden chair, and tugged it toward me, scraping a pile of ash-colored wood chips from its seat to the floor.

"Rose and her boyfriend, Robert, live in the front. I'm Stuart Harwood, and this is my studio..." waving an arm, proudly displaying his work- and living-space.

It was a high-ceilinged loft, painted white, with a sink and an electric hotplate on a crate, forming a tiny kitchen. The front of the huge room was a walled-off space with two small rooms—now sublet, I was delighted to learn, by Rose and Robert. A long wooden workbench took up most of the rear wall facing the door. It was littered from end to end with tools and miscellaneous articles of whatever uses, I had no idea. The high, wide wall alongside the door I'd entered was hung with a fabulous collage of objects, including pictures clipped from magazines, nature scenes, the works of famous sculptors and painters, whitened bones, leather and metal bits of harness, newspaper clippings, charcoal sketches, a variety of battered hats—mostly stuff gleaned from the city's bountiful streets.

"Have some coffee! Rose should be home any minute now." Stuart poured me a cup of coffee from a grey enamel pot— thick, black and oft-reheated. "I'm a sculptor," he sounded proud, and sure of this identity. "I came here last January from San Francisco, to get my work seen. San Francisco's a great town, but the market is here."

As I sipped very cautiously at my bitter, lukewarm coffee, he moved around his space with restless, buoyant energy, sometimes picking up the mallet and gouge he'd been using before I came, as if itching to get back to it. The piece he was carving was a seven-foot-long ash-and-cream-colored log, resting on two homemade sawhorses. He said the wood had been a train-track crosspiece he'd unearthed from the mud of the East Riverbank in Brooklyn.

"This is ironwood—they used it for its toughness and endurance. See how the iron bolts that fastened it down have bled into the wood, from grey to black, at the ends of this beautiful piece? I've found a bunch of these over there, and some gorgeous teak logs." With a few deft blows from the mallet, he sliced a handful of slender spoon-shaped chunks from the center of the log.

This guy, I thought, doesn't seem to need any encouragement from me to keep him talking; though he looked into my face often, his shining blue eyes showing nothing but delight at my unexpected presence. I was suddenly very glad that I had worn my favorite yellow cotton shirt with thin multi-colored stripes to work that day.

"I'm always amazed at the stuff people throw out—I find most of my material at the dump, or on the street—like this great old armchair"—a large brown relic with frayed binding on its nearly flat cushion; he brushed a fond hand over its oily-looking back but didn't sit down—I wondered if he ever sat down.

He picked up a handful wood chips and gestured toward a pot-bellied stove that sat on a brick foundation near the improvised "kitchen."

"I nearly froze to death last winter! When I first got here, I didn't know anything about really cold weather!" He laughed at his foolhardy ignorance: "I've lived in California, and Florida and Guam and the Palau Islands—I just didn't know I'd need really warm clothes, and hats and overcoats and gloves—and heat!" He tossed in the chips in the small stove—"but I'll be warm this winter!"

Ignorant though I was about dating in general, I knew that men tend to talk non-stop about themselves—though I'd never been the recipient of so much energy and passion in the telling; but this Stuart Harwood, after tossing a handful of wood chips into the stove door, leaned back against his workbench and began asking me questions about myself—with real curiosity and interest. I'd never met anyone so fascinated by my unprepossessing, bookish self.

(I hadn't yet grasped that this intriguing, talented man was as lonely and isolated in this exciting city as I was.)

He wanted to know how I knew Rose, how many brothers

and sisters I had (one brother, to his three brothers and two sisters), what Missouri is like, what I studied in college—"a Masters in Philosophy! Wow!"—details of my job at Bellevue Hospital, my tastes in music, art, books. . .

Then back to his own story, as if he wanted me to know everything about him, instantly.

"I never went to college, except for a few months in art school on the GI Bill—but they threw me out—I wouldn't do everything it said in the rulebooks—not conventional enough!" He grinned proudly at this achievement; but I caught an under-current of regret, even a tad of shame, that he'd missed out on college.

"I was in the Air Force for four years—but they wouldn't let me fly, their tests showed I could never kill anybody—and after the war I got into carpentry. At twenty-three, I became the youngest general contractor in California! We put up house frames by the hundreds, made money—but it seemed meaning-less, it wasn't for me."

He grinned, holding up his right hand, which had a shiny bump where the index finger had been. "Lost this under a house when I passed out, while holding an electric saw above me! Lucky I didn't drop it on my stomach!

"I taught myself sculpture in Palau. I'd joined the Seabees during the Korean War, built quarters for the troops in Guam and Palau. The islanders'd bring me pieces of these beautiful native hardwoods to carve—the guys thought I was crazy! I started out making salt-and-pepper shakers—but then I got into making larger carvings, that kept getting more abstract—at first, I didn't know I was making sculpture! But I kept on with it after I got back, and—just before I came here, I had some pieces in a show in San Francisco! They got a rave review from Alfred Frankenstein, the famous art critic for the *Chronicle*! Here, I'll show you . . ." He grabbed a paper-stuffed wallet from the littered workbench and found a carefully folded clipping of a favorable critique of several of his works.

More than slightly dazed by this very attractive, garrulous, gifted dynamo, I watched and listened, fascinated, not even slightly anxious for Rose and Robert to show up. He'd found a broom and made a stab at tidying the floor as he described his harsh Depression-era childhood:

"We lived in San Diego—six little towheaded stair-steps—I was the second oldest to my brother, Howard. Our father, Rendell Bickford"—a shadow dimmed his blue eyes for a moment—"I've got no use for him—that's why I use 'Harwood,' my mom's maiden name, and my grandma's name, 'Stuart.' He abandoned us when the youngest, Rick, was on the way. We lived on thirty dollars a month from Welfare—there was never enough to eat—so most of the others got rickets or TB—but I'd go into the cans behind restaurants and eat what other people wasted.

"And I always had a job, from the age of nine—I'd sweep out stores, and they'd give me a nickel or a piece of candy."

Scooping chips and other bits of miscellaneous litter into an improvised dustpan, he skimmed over his early marriage:

"We were both nineteen—way too young. I joined the Air Force to fly, but spent the whole war in Florida, testing pilots' tolerance in pressure chambers—but my wife was too afraid to leave her mother and come to live with me." He proudly showed me snapshots of his two beautiful small blond daughters, who lived in California with their mother and stepfather.

"We got divorced right after the war." His face briefly lost its glow as he murmured, "I miss those babies so much!" His chin wobbled slightly and then hardened as he stopped moving for a moment, looked at the worn Chronicle clipping, and proclaimed—defiantly, I thought—"The Work comes first!"

Time was flying by—I'd almost forgotten about his tardy

housemates, as Stuart shared his tenets on creating wood sculpture (while rinsing dishes in his tiny sink): "People don't understand wood, they think it's blocky, chunky—they carve big hunks that crack and split—they don't see that it's like strings glued together; its strength is tensile strength—as in a violin bow, or a berry box. I use the long grain of the wood to express its delicacy and strength at the same time."

Finally, at about nine-thirty, they came through the door, Rose and her Robert, a thin, dark-haired young man with thick spectacles and a slightly puzzled expression. Rose seemed pleased to see me, though we'd never really been friends at school, and she suggested that I stay for dinner. We had a delicious meal of spaghetti and homemade tomato sauce, French bread and Chianti; Rose and I described our more hilariously absurd philosophy professors for the men's delight, everyone talked and laughed—just as I had assumed sophisticated New Yorkers would do. It was, by a Missouri mile, the best evening I'd spent up to then, in New York—or anywhere else, come to think of it.

At two in the morning, Stuart walked me through the rough but quiet streets to the subway at Fourteenth Street. He never let up—or ran down! The smile, the warmth, the fascinating narrative. We parted with a warm handshake—but I didn't realize till later that he didn't ask me for my phone number.

I had a lonesome Thanksgiving Day, with a rare, expensive phone call to my family in Miami. My days resumed, still hopeful, with small new adventures in the scintillating city, and the addition of a bright, a bit weird, but happy memory.

John

Only a couple of weeks later, out of the blue, I received a thick letter from John Collier, Junior, a former grad student/painting major, a peripheral member of our little "band of aesthetes," as one of our professors called the few philosophy, art, literature and music students who hung out together in our free time.

John had impressed me with his pastel abstract-impressionist oils, and even more when he left the U shortly before receiving his Masters, on grounds that a serious painter didn't need a degree. At that time, though, dropping out made him fair game for the Armed Forces, and he'd written to me from an Army camp in Georgia.

John, who came from a well-to-do Texas family, was the only one of our small crowd with any discretionary money, beyond an occasional pitcher of 3.2 beer. He had his own studio-like apartment above a store on Main Street in Columbia, where he sometimes gave little parties—with no furniture other than his mattress on the floor, and a wooden table on which there'd be wine, cheeses and, what had delighted me the most, a silver vase of white, heavenly-smelling freesias. *Don Giovanni* on the stereo, friends and wine—it had all seemed so sophisticated. But I didn't really know him, nor he me; we'd had two dates, that never went beyond some shy hugging and kissing. I had not thought about him once, since leaving school.

His letter said that he was coming to New York on his ten-day Christmas leave, he'd like to see me—and he thought that he might like to marry me! He sounded serious—John always sounded serious.

Astonished, I dropped the pages on the floor of my tiny bed-sit and roared at the absurdity of it!

You'll understand how lonely I had become in the past six

months, when I admit that, after another cold, joyless week or two of dismal typing and filing, riding the filthy subway packed with belligerent, combative citizens—and not even fifty cents left over to go to the Museum of Modern Art, after paying my thirteen dollars' weekly rent—I wrote and invited him to come. I'd get him a room in my building, and then—we would see!

John came, tall and pale in his khaki uniform, wearing his clear- rimmed glasses; he was, in fact, a handsome young man with perfectly clean fingernails, polite and, like me, excited at this outrageous experiment we were making. My parents, who also seemed to be jazzed by my having a (solvent) boyfriend, sent me back the $400 I had been mailing to them at $25 a month since I'd got a job, and I bought us cheap tickets to a few Broadway shows. On our first weekend I showed him the sights I knew he'd love—the famous art museums and galleries, with one extended subway ride to the Cloisters, full of ancient tapestries and paintings. His room was on the floor below mine, and, good little 50's children that we were, we maintained our separate quarters at night, after a hug and a kiss at parting.

By the end of a week spent together, except for my working hours, John and I felt a bit closer—we'd shared more about our families, our histories, our hopes—the most immediate, that his first year-long tour of duty with the U.S. Occupying Forces would take him (and possibly me) to Japan, rather than Germany. He was almost rhapsodic about Japanese art, their gardens and architecture—while to me, the mere idea of crossing an ocean to another country seemed like a wonderful dream come true.

We had three days left—it took that long to get blood tests for a marriage license—but an elderly doctor friend at Bellevue arranged for us to get a quickie test—and then, on a Tuesday afternoon, we took a bus down to City Hall and got married. I had a green-and-yellow orchid corsage on the shoulder of my old brown suit, and my groom was dressed in civvies and a tie as we stood before the insanely pontifical clerk who married us with a flourish.

On our way back down the great grey and white marble stairway, John stopped for a moment, looked away from me and said quietly, "I wonder if we're making a terrible mistake."

So did I, but it seemed like a tactless time to say so.

During one of the three days he remained in the city, I took John to East Tenth Street to meet Stuart Harwood. The two artists seemed to hit it off well, though our marriage was a big surprise to the sculptor. He laughed ruefully, saying that he had got my phone number from Rose, but it didn't work—one digit wrong, as he eventually learned—and he had tried to find me at Bellevue, where they claimed to have no listing of my minuscule presence. John asked him if he would "watch out for me" after he left town, and he said he'd be happy to; they even promised to exchange a painting for a sculpture when we were finally able to go on with our domestic and creative lives.

Despite what John and I considered our liberal views on society in general, we had not slept together until we were "properly" hitched; and during the last two nights, we cuddled. But though he made a concerted effort, he did not get an erection. That didn't alarm me; I'd had little experience with sex—one brief affair in college—and John didn't seem to have much more than I did. I put it down to the stress of our life-changing decision and the mad rush to carry it out. We would need time together, of course, which would only come with his settling into our new home, wherever that might be, and then sending for me to join him.

After John left, I felt much more alone than before—scared, fragile, anxiously waiting for word from him—which did not come for three weeks. When at last I received a brief letter, it stated, with no sentimentality nor gentleness to cushion the brutal clarity of his words:

"I don't want to be married, after all. It was a terrible mistake; let's forget it."

It was hardly a complete surprise—his words to me after our "wedding," and the endless wait for any communication from him after he'd left, had produced on me a kind of defensive shell; I had my whole little universe of family and friends to answer to. I had to keep my pride, somehow or other. Moreover, I had always believed that when you got married, you made a life-long commitment, a union created as a foundation for a full, productive life. In short, I was a real dope. I had convinced myself that I loved him—sort of—and that all we needed was more time together.

I wrote to him every day, eloquent, affectionate letters (he had been, as he'd hoped, posted to Kyoto, Japan) to convince him that we should at least give it a try.

Meanwhile, my family assumed that things were moving along happily, the people at my new job were excited for me, and his friends and relations were loading his parents with a ton of fancy, useless stuff, to keep for us until we had a home. In her frequent, gushing letters to me, his mother duly described each gift in detail, so that I could send proper little thank you notes to those nice, well-heeled Texans for their lovely Wedgwood tea services, crystal goblets, silver coffee urns, linen table-cloth-and-napkin sets. I felt like a not-very-well-trained seal, trying to keep too many balls in the air.

But my chief preoccupation was preparing to go to Japan. I'd left Bellevue when my stone-faced supervisor refused to give me a day off to get married, but I'd found a much better job, as secretary in an intercultural organization called American Friends of the Middle East. We worked in a gracious four-story house on East Sixty-seventh Street, where conditions, working hours, co-workers and salary were, to me, much more copacetic. Unknown to anyone, except John, I'd booked passage on a freighter for early May, and I was even able to save a bit of money for my trip, and for the required shots for typhus, cholera and yellow fever. I made some good friends there at AFME, including, weirdly enough, a sweet British girl, Brenda, who told me that her boyfriend was a sculptor named Stuart Harwood (!)—and that he was showing some of his work at a gallery near our offices!

So, one chilly March evening, after work, I walked over to the gallery: a large, light-filled space with the sculptures of several artists displayed on a series of ascending platforms. I saw Harwood's piece—a tall, graceful, spiraling column of ivory-colored wood, blending at the ends into soft grey, tapering tips. It stood there in calm beauty and serenity, like a column of smoke, about to waft skyward and disappear. Its delicate beauty, and its natural rightness, hit me in the pit of the stomach, like a Rembrandt self-portrait or an El Greco landscape. A masterpiece.

So: that glib, smiling, blond hunk was this—a man who could carve into being something so pure and so true! This work was in a different class from the self-conscious productions of the other artists in the show—or, indeed, in the many gallery shows I'd seen in New York. Who was he, really, that he could do this?

I wrote him a postcard, that night, with a short paean of praise, and two days later he called, overjoyed at my comprehension of his work. He invited me to go with him to the ballet—as he reminded me, he had promised John to "look after me." And he asked me to call him "Merrill" as a sign of friendship.

We both loved the ballet; then we crossed Fifty-Seventh Street to the Russian Tea Room, where we talked for hours, each of us moved to find the other richly thoughtful, humorous and empathetic.

I didn't tell him about the situation with John; I had told no one. I was still denying it to myself—writing him urgent, reassuring letters every day. He had begun to respond, reluctant and agitated, saying that he'd made arrangements for our housing there, and he'd ordered two silk dresses to be made for me in Hong Kong. He described the great beauty of Kyoto, and sent me two Japanese prints to hang on my bare walls. But then, one afternoon, he had called me at work, sobbing, to beg me not to come; he said that if I did, he'd tell the army not to let me stay. I think that, by that point, the lure of the voyage and its exotic destination made me more determined to go than ever —and let the chips fall as they would.

Early one beautiful Saturday morning in April, Merrill phoned to invite me to go with him to search the bank of the East River for wood to carve; he'd rented a truck and would pick me up in an hour. But it happened that our first stop, at the Brooklyn home of a carpenter friend of his, involved emptying, a bucket at a time, many gallons of water from a used water heater, so that Merrill could un-plumb the thing and install it in his cold-water loft. Next, we drove to a riverside dump, where we marveled at the great stuff people toss out. (We salvaged a very old, undamaged bent-wood coat rack that we used for many years.)

Then we ate oysters at Original Joe's, and finally, made a cursory hunt for wooden treasure on the soggy riverbank, where no promising logs were that day evident. I hadn't had so much fun for years.

I mused that this fellow sure knew how to give a girl a good time!

Neither of us wanted to go home; it was still a perfect spring afternoon; we had wheels and could take ourselves to some grassy spot in the countryside, well away from the concrete city. We crossed the George Washington Bridge to New Jersey, where after an hour's drive through industrial wastelands, we finally stopped by a stream, which, though polluted and innocent of all but some yellowish vegetation, offered a place where we could sit and talk.

Finally, after we had each drunk a lukewarm beer, my defenses collapsed. I described my lonely struggle of the past four months, the letters, the wedding gifts, and the frantic rejection in my last message from John. I wept, just a little, and Merrill became very tender. Then he told me that, though he would never have interfered in a viable marriage—as it was *not*... and we kissed, for the first time. But lightly.

Still unwilling to say goodbye, we drove back to his loft. (By good fortune, Ruth and Robert had moved on by this time.) We talked, made dinner; talked some more—and somewhere around midnight, I recited for him my favorite poem, Gerard Manley Hopkins' "The Windhover":

> *I caught this morning morning's minion,*
> *kingdom of daylight's dauphin*
> *in his riding of the rolling level, underneath him,*
> *steady air,*
> *and, riding high there,*
> *how he wrung upon the wing of a wimpling*
> *wind in his ecstasy !...*

A disaster! Hopkins turned out to be too much for both of us. We fell into each other' arms, trembling, ecstatic, amazed. But still, kind of innocent. We went to bed in separate rooms; but sometime later, I called out and he came to me. For the first time in my life, I made love—tender, caring, thrilling love—and was made love to.

But I was still headed to Japan.

On Monday, the staff of AFME ate lunch together in the roomy kitchen, as usual. Such occasions were ordinarily pleasant chances to chit-chat and shop-talk, but this day, one of the publicity staff, a charming, witty older woman whom I greatly admired, began, for some unknown reason, to tell the dramatic story of her blissful twenty-year marriage. She said she had been married, quite contentedly, to another man, when she sat down beside a stranger at a professional banquet. They had, she said, immediately fallen madly in love, left their respective spouses, and married one another. They had never regretted a thing.

At that moment I realized that I was never, ever going to Japan. I cancelled my voyage and showed up at East Tenth Street that evening with a huge bunch of lilacs.

So we began our lives together.

Crossing Back

It was 1957, the end of our year-long honeymoon in Italy, courtesy of Merrill's Fulbright Scholarship. We had lived in Florence, where he was, technically, enrolled at the *Istituto d'Arte*, but in truth, spent most days hanging out at a tiny foundry that he had discovered on his own. He was learning to cast bronze, as Michelangelo, his idolized paragon, had done, by the ancient lost-wax process. His *professore* was a grizzled workman in grimy overalls, named Aldo, who, in exchange learned American cusswords.

I had imagined that I'd spend a lot of my "free time" writing, but I soon found that it took half the day to walk to the *Mercato Centrale*, buy milk, fruit, eggs, vegetables, a bit of meat, tomato sauce and pasta, all at separate stalls, lug it all home in string bags, and cook dinner on a two-burner hot plate.

Our kitchen, with a rough floor of *pietra serena*—the grey granite from which most buildings in Florence had been constructed, centuries before—was once the greenhouse of a three-story villa—now converted into several apartments. Our jovial landlord, the Marchese Fioravanti, welcomed Fulbright scholars and artists as temporary tenants at roof-top cocktail parties, where he instructed a young boy in a starched white coat to "spray the legs" (*tutte le gambe*) of all the guests with mosquito killer.

It soon became evident that trying to write in our chilly, damp, bed/sitting room, which was also Merrill's sculpture "studio," was not nearly so rewarding as taking a bus—any bus —from the central piazza, to one of the city's sunny surrounding hills, or reading every Henry James novel at the U.S. Information Service Library. Or seducing my handsome husband, from whom I fiercely desired a baby.

The after-effects of World War II were still very evident in

Florence, as well as in the other Italian cities we visited. In Rome, where we exchanged apartments with another Fulbright couple for a week in May, bombing ruins were still visible in many places, some even scattered among the cherished ruins of ancient times. Post-war Florence was a place of genteel poverty, where women hurried to their jobs in offices or shops, wearing neatly brushed woolen suits and high heels, but with angry-looking chilblains on their legs from their unheated homes or workplaces.

There was a limited selection of merchandise in the shops, and little traffic from cars or trucks; riders had converted tiny Vespas into haulers of huge stacks of goods or lumber, by rigging them with platforms on the vehicles' backs and over their heads.

Though many struggling Italians considered Merrill and me "rich Americans," we were poor, and used to poverty—ours being, we liked to think, more Bohemian than genteel. At twenty-four, I was still wearing clothes from high school and college, patched and mended when necessary. In Merrill's East Village loft In New York, we'd considered ourselves wealthy from the bounty of furniture, tools, wood and even marble that others threw away.

Very little got thrown out in Italy in those days—but, except for the clothes, which I couldn't possibly afford, goods were relatively inexpensive. We were two adults living on a stipend of $100 a month, with little to spend on anything but necessities, but we managed to eat well, and we frequented the inexpensive museums. We even went to the opera every week, during the season, for fifty cents each, where we sat on hard bleachers and joined in the bravos and catcalls from the audience, many of whom knew the libretti and sang along with the soloists.

We were in complete agreement that money was no big

deal, except for necessities—but Art was essential, and Love was paramount! Even so, I found it hard, sometimes, to look in the shop windows and see elegant leather goods, or exquisitely embroidered linens, with no possibility of owning any of them.

When my parents sent me fifty dollars for my birthday—30,000 lire, in those days!—Merrill insisted that I spend it on anything I wanted, which sent me into a panic, imagining the treasures I could buy!

It took a while, but I finally decided on a big, golden-brown leather handbag with a zipper compartment between two large pockets. It was heavy, even when empty—but I thought about how many things it could carry—even, I hoped and prayed, baby gear. It was the most gorgeous object I'd ever owned, and I was grateful to Merrill, as well as my folks, for insisting that I indulge myself with all that money!

I'd also got a birthday card from my Aunt Iris with a five-dollar bill—but that, he grabbed away from me, laughing, "You'll lose that!"

He tucked it into his billfold, saying, "We'll keep it for emergencies."

Okay by me.

Merrill was generous with everything he had—a warm, funny, and very sensual man. As a lover, he brought me the sweetness of being half of a joyful, happy creature. Our sexual appetites were so well matched, that I marveled that many women—at least in novels and movies—were cold or passive with their partners. The soft, golden hair of his chest and forearms, or the curve of his naked back as he bent over a piece he was carving, made me crave him so fiercely that I had to force myself to go outside and let him work.

But now, our wondrous Year-of Not-Having-to Work-at-Some-Boring-Job-for-a-Living (bless Senator Fulbright!) had come to an end. We had saved some money, hoping to travel a bit on our way back to Southampton, England, and the ten days' voyage home on the *Ile de France*.

It was November; the leaves on the chestnut trees in Paris glowed amber; warm, sun-kissed days ended in cool, romantic evenings on the Seine. We supposed. But *we* were both—serially-- sick as dogs! A few days before we left Florence, we'd learned that I was pregnant, and though wild with joy, I had the kind of "morning sickness" that lasts all day, every day, and invites vomiting into any handy receptacle.

By the time we reached Paris on the train, I was too weak and sick to do any sight-seeing—much less, savor the local cuisine—and I had to subsist on the bread and soup that Merrill carried up the six flights to our gritty little room on the Left Bank. For two days, he went out, alone, to see Paris—the Louvre, the Orangerie, a Rodin exhibit—returning to describe to me the sweeping expanse and grandeur of the *Champs-Elysees*, the manicured beauty of the *Tuileries* gardens. But on the third morning, he complained of a severe headache, nausea, and muscular pain. We recognized the symptoms of Asian flu—an epidemic in Europe that year. I don't remember my treks up and down those six flights of marble stairs, but I must have managed to go for provisions. Although my poor boy couldn't keep anything down, I, despite my perpetual nausea, was so ravenous that I would eat anything that the shopkeeper, contemptuous of my junior-college French, rolled up for me in his little paper cone.

After two more days of Parisian purgatory, we crawled back onto the train, and, in due course, embarked upon the tossing and heaving English Channel. There, at least, we were only two of many people hanging their throbbing heads over the ship's rail.

We reached Southampton just in time to get to the port and go through Customs before sailing; my leather bag was all we had to declare. (Merrill's bronze-and-marble sculpture had been carefully crated and shipped before we left Florence.) But the British Customs inspector glanced at my passport and politely pointed out that it had expired two months before!

I grabbed Merrill's arm.

"Oh. no! I got it two years ago for that trip to Japan that I never took!" (I thought, but didn't say, *"because I moved in with you instead of taking a freighter to Japan to join a brand-new husband who had just figured out that he was gay and didn't want me, thank the Lord!"*)

My gorgeous, current husband, who really did want me, gave me a hug and turned to the official with his most engaging smile.

"Can't you let us through, sir? Our ship is just about to sail, and we don't have time to get a new passport—but we absolutely *must* be on that ship!"

Indeed, we did. Our passage had been paid by the Fulbright—and we were flat broke!

"No, I'm very sorry, sir, no one can embark without a valid passport. I suggest you go to the American Consulate—it's only five minutes away by foot."

Ah, yes, we'd heard that the American Consulate was the place to go if you got into trouble abroad—but how could we possibly do all that in the half hour before the ship sailed? Short of sneaking aboard and hiding in a lifeboat during our voyage to New York, we had no choice but to try. The official gave us directions, and we trotted the short distance, with as much speed as we could muster, after our sickly week in Paris.

We were immediately ushered into an office and seen by a well-groomed middle-aged man, who terrified us by first stating —rather brutally—that it would take a full day to issue a new passport. However, he added, if we had a photo of me, it could be affixed to Merrill's passport, and cover us both—and it would only cost five dollars!

"Oh, hey, yeah—I've got one!" Merrill took out his battered wallet and found therein a small high-school graduation photo of me, looking beautiful and sultry (not much like me at all, but perfectly adequate for the purpose). He grinned as he handed it to the Consul—but then he turned to me with a deep groan.

"But, honey—*we don't have any money!* We spent every last cent getting here from Paris!" He turned back to the diplomat, looking like poor little Oliver Twist as he pleaded with the man.

"Please, sir, could you possibly advance us the five dollars? We'll send it back to you as soon as we get home!"

I recalled with some relief that we had, providentially, left $200 in a bank in New York. (*And we would have sent the money, whatever you, reader, or the Consular man might think!*). But then, I suddenly remember my gentle husband grabbing a bill out of my hand . . .

"Oh, hey, Babe, remember? Aunt Iris's five-dollar emergency stash! Look in your wallet—if *this* isn't an emergency ...!"

"Umm—yeah," he frowned. He retrieved his wallet, pulling from it a wad of dog-eared papers and cards--which proved to be its entire contents. He shook his head in despair.

"Guess I lost it, hon."

"Oh, *no*, now what do we do?" I looked helplessly to the official—and then at his metal wastebasket, which my stomach felt might be required at any moment now.

The gentleman looked at us with mild reproach, but graciously refrained from saying what he thought of people who managed to be penniless in a foreign country.

"It's not really a problem," he said kindly. He took a brush from a small glue-pot, and pasted my picture into Merrill's passport, then wrote and stamped the required information. He handed it back to Merrill.

"You'll just make your ship if you hurry."

We burbled our thanks to the kind man and hurried back to the Customs shed. We were the last passengers aboard.

After the great liner had pulled out of the harbor, and we had been fed a sumptuous French meal such as we could never have afforded in France—if we could have stomached it—we strolled to our tiny, shared cabin, where we had an upper and a lower bunk. We sat on the lower, and Merrill put his arm around me.

"People have been very nice to us, haven't they?" I murmured, muzzling into his warm neck.

"They sure have, honey. We'd have been in a hell of a mess without them." He took my hand and squeezed it.

"Janny, I have to tell you something. . ."

I looked into his sky-blue eyes with adoration—my darling, my child's father-to be.

"Why, what is it, love?"

He looked away. "I spent the five bucks in Paris."

"Oh, is that all? That's okay, sweetie. But why didn't you tell me?"

"I went to a girlie show—when you were sick—before *I* was." His forehead was flushed and damp.

"*You* went to a *girlie show*, when I was sick in bed with our unborn baby. While I was puking my guts out in that miserable little room."

My voice was low and even.

"I'm really, really sorry! I was too ashamed to tell you."

"Did it turn you on? Was it really sexy?"

"No, not really. It was pretty shoddy and stupid."

I stood up, careful not to bang my head on the upper bunk.

"I need to go to bed now. I hope I'm not sick the whole way over."

He grabbed my hand as I moved toward the minuscule bathroom.

"Baby, are we okay?"

I put both hands on his flushed cheeks, sighed and kissed his forehead.

"Your first time in Paris, you go to a girlie show. I guess that's normal."

I was so tired, I wanted to pull the covers over my head and sleep for the whole ten days of the crossing.

The Cuban Crisis in New Jersey

October 16-29, 1962

While it was still dark, Merrill carried Rachel down the stairs to the kitchen, folded over his shoulder, limp as a sack of corn-meal. He set her down gently on a wool army blanket near the potbellied stove. I was close by in the rocking chair, nursing six-month-old Ben.

I felt bruised from my efforts with the breast pump. I'd expressed enough milk for two days. The bottles of thin, yellowish liquid were in the refrigerator, but this morning, I felt an overwhelming need for intimate communion with my baby.

Rachel, three-and-a-half, fell backward against her father's chest as he knelt to pull on her corduroy overalls. He nuzzled her soft, tangled hair as he guided her foot through a pants leg. She mumbled something, still half asleep.

"What'd you say, sweetheart?"

"Where is Mama going?" Her eyes were still shut tight.

"How do you know she's going somewhere, pussycat?"

Merrill raised his eyebrows at me. I shrugged, grinning in spite of my discomfort from the baby's desperate sucking at my swollen nipple.

"Maybe she heard me on the phone with Warren."

He drew Rachel's arms through the sleeves of her pink sweater, one after the other. He kissed her small retroussé nose.

"Mama's going on a little trip today, to Washington D.C., to picket the White House, with a lot of other people. We're going to drive her to the train station—and you'll get to see the train!"

Her hazel eyes opened wide at that, and she bounded over to my chair, laying her head on my arm. "Can I go with you, Mama? I want to go on the train!"

I shifted Ben to my other breast and pulled Rachel closer.

"Not this time, sugar. You need to stay and help daddy take care of the boys."

"But I want to go-o-o-o!" She wailed, burrowing her head in my loose cotton shirt.

My tears threatened, but I blinked them back hard.

"I know, honey! This is the first time I've gone anywhere without you, and I don't like it, either! But I'll be back home by tomorrow afternoon."

I fervently hoped I wasn't wrong. It seemed way too melo-dramatic, bizarre even to think it, but I, like millions of people, both Americans and Russians—knew that it was perfectly possible that I might never see any of my precious family again after today.

Merrill found our two-year-old—Garth, whom we called by his middle name, Davy, in his crib, just hoisting a leg over the top rail. At two-and-a-half, he could climb out with little effort, and he had a couple of bruised knees to show for it.

"Hey, hold on there, pardner," Merrill called, rushing to pick up the adventurous boy, whose luminous eyes, a shade of hazel lighter than his sister's, beamed with delight in this new day.

Merrill swung him up and galloped piggyback down to the kitchen. I'd set Ben on the army blanket, where he was grunting with the effort to get his knees under him. Rachel sat beside him, pulling her red socks on.

"I'm hungry!" Davy announced, "I want Rice Krispies!"

"Well, good morning to you, too, honeybunch!"

I took a quick mental snapshot of my tall, grinning husband, with a much smaller, rosy face rising above his own. Merrill somersaulted Davy, whooping with glee, over his head and down into my arms. I gave him a thorough smooch before handing him back to his dad.

"You can have a banana now, Davy, but we have to hurry, to take me to the train—Daddy can give you cereal when you get back home."

"We goin' on a *train?*" He jumped with excitement, so that Merrill had to grab a handful of his pajama pants to hold him steady.

"No, Davy," Rachel answered with authority. "*We* can't go. Mama's going to pick at the White House."

"What house? I'm goin' too, Mama!"

"Don't worry, sport, I'm taking care of you today," Merrill said.

"Hey, hold still a minute!" He pulled a t-shirt over the child's head, careful to stretch the neck.

"Okay, well, I guess I'm ready." I stood up, noticing that the baby blanket had left a drift of lint on the front of my navy skirt. I licked my fingers and brushed at it, quivering with suppressed panic and the need to get going—*but how can I bear to leave you? You guys are everything to me... I just want to sit here on the floor all day and let you climb all over me...*

I said, "I'll bring the car around."

Merrill took two bananas from a bowl on the kitchen table and handed one to each child. "I'll be right back," he told them, rushing to the door in time to catch me juggling my purse, an overnight bag, and a long-stemmed placard proclaiming: SAVE THE CHILDREN—NO NUCLEAR WAR!

I'd arranged to spend that night with our friends, the Franklins, in Manhattan, since there'd be no train connection to Sussex until the next morning... *if trains and towns still existed by then.*

"Let me take that stuff, Jan," Merrill called. I handed the bag and the sign to him, but he set them down and took me by the shoulders, looking intently into my face. My long brown hair was pulled into a more-or-less tidy ponytail. I wore no makeup and I'd seen the dark smudges under my eyes from the strain of the past few terrible weeks. I recalled once, in our early days together, when he had looked at me just that way, saying, "I think your face looks exactly the way a face ought to look."

I hoped that he still thought so.

"I know you've got to do this."

"Of course! *What else can I do?*" Fury burst out of me: "But how could this be happening? Those men are all insane! Don't they have kids at home?"

Merrill folded his arms around me and held me hard against him. With his face buried in my hair, he muttered, "I know—how could our country—*our world*—have come to this? But listen, hon, things could still happen: Khrushchev might back down, Kennedy could decide to hold off and negotiate . . . *Don't give up!*"

"Not until I have no choice."

We kissed with intensity. Then we got moving.

"The kids can help me clean up in the garden today . . . and, of course, I know what to do if there's an alert."

Our rented farmhouse had no basement, but there was a deep concrete-lined cellar in the empty main house just across the road. Our landlord had allowed us to stock it with canned food, water, candles, matches and blankets, but we had very little faith in this makeshift "fall-out shelter." We were living in the midst of verdant pastureland and apple orchards, sixty miles north of Manhattan—but we knew that our chances of survival were nil if there were a nuclear attack on New York City.

All through the past two weeks, the nation had listened to the radio and television with increasing horror, as the "unthinkable"—Herman Kahn's term for his coldly calculated outcome of the "Cold War"—had become more "thinkable" every day. I'd lain awake night after night, trying to imagine how the children and I could cope, and for how long—probably without Merrill.

He had been a rising young abstract sculptor in New York when we met, but after the babies started coming, he'd found work as a sheet-metal fabricator in Dover, thirty-five miles south of us. After an attack, even if he was alive, he might not be able to get to us. But, meanwhile, we couldn't afford for him to miss work!

I sometimes woke up in a panic, sweating, heart pounding. Nobody had good answers: if the blast didn't kill us all instantly, how long could we stay alive—and would we want to live when we emerged into a Hiroshima-gray world of poisoned air, fire and burned-out debris?

I often told myself that we would never have brought these infinitely dear little people into the world, if we hadn't been so ignorant about the ways that the strutting masters of our fragile world were playing the nuclear threat to control each other.

Merrill and I had been politically naïve, and quite comfortably so, until our new friends, Camilla and Warren Greenleaf, found out how little we knew about world affairs. For several months, they'd been supplying us with back issues of *The Nation, I.F. Stone's Weekly*, and *The Progressive*. We were horrified at what we learned from these left leaning but fiercely democratic publications.

After absorbing the contents of dozens of the magazines, I had phoned the Greenleafs' rustic home in the woods near Flatbrookville.

"But, come *on*, Warren! Can there *possibly be* an *official government policy called MAD?*"

Warren assured me that "Mutually Assured Destruction" was the stated aim of our country's huge nuclear build-up: to paralyze the Soviet Union so that they wouldn't dare to use their A-bombs against us.

He was in his sixties, a rotund, usually mirthful Irish-American political writer, who with his brilliant historian wife had retired to rural New Jersey to write long-planned books. They'd been our closest neighbors, some eight miles away, when Merrill and I moved from New York to a tiny cottage on the banks of the Delaware River, seeking a peaceful place to raise our first child. Our two couples, so diverse in age, had become dear friends, as we all shared a passion for books, music, art and simple, natural living. In the past year, we had moved our growing family to a larger house, some twenty miles away over the Pocono foothills, but we still made visits back and forth, and the Greenleafs were delighted to act as occasional substitute grandparents.

Though a Democrat and a political progressive, Warren was suffused by a long-held rage against the Soviet Union. He nearly shouted into the phone: "I've been telling them for years —the Communists are *determined to destroy us*—they always have been! 'Way back in the Thirties I told my knee-jerk liberal friends that they were dupes to join the Party—and look what happened to *them! Disgraced!* Blackballed from their careers, driven to leave the country, or to find inferior work here."

"So, maybe they do want to destroy us," I conceded, but there must be a better response than turning the world into a nuclear fireball!"

"I agree with you there, my dear. Both nations have fallen into a deadly quagmire of their own making, and nobody seems able to figure a way out of it."

I'd been hoping for a more positive response, wise and diplomatic—something that might make all this terrible new knowledge more human, more graspable from a mother's point of view.

"But, *why, why do we all just sit still* for this? There must be something we can do! If people only realized what's hanging over all our heads . . ."

"The people, as always, are determined to be ignorant of facts they don't want to know . . . Hold on, Jan, Camilla wants to talk to you."

His wife's kind, cultured voice came over the wire.

"Jan? I'm sorry our magazines upset you, dear. I had no idea you'd be so stricken—we've been following all this for years and considered it general knowledge."

"Oh, Camilla, I'm so glad we know! We were so stupid. We just thought about babies, art and books and lovely things—and now! I wish I could think of some way to help— being so *help-less* terrifies me!"

"There are anti-nuclear groups you could join—they put meeting notices in the magazines. And you can write letters to the local papers! You've got a fine brain, Jan—I think it will make you feel much better to start using it for something besides childcare, important as that is."

In early spring, I wrote to the Committee for a Sane Nuclear Policy, "SANE," offering to do typing for them, or anything else I could do from my home. A few days later, a woman with a businesslike voice phoned me from national SANE headquarters.

"Well, why not start a chapter out there? You say you're isolated, but I'm sure you'd find like-minded people. Put a notice in the local paper."

We had met very few people in the local community. Our nearest neighbors, half-a-mile away, were small dairy farmers. The Hauptmans were a large, hearty family with three sturdy teenagers, who were pleased when I took the children to watch at milking time. Mrs. Hauptman showed me how to preserve the delicious little brown pears from our tree. But she had no interest in politics.

"It's terrible what you say, Mrs. Harwood, but *we* don't have anything to do with such things. I guess the government knows what it's doing. Just so the Russians don't come and take our farm away!"

I was doubtful about getting a more enlightened response from our rural neighbors, but Merrill was all for the idea. We sent a notice to newspapers in several nearby towns, inviting anyone who was concerned about the nuclear threat to a meeting at a local church.

To my amazement, a dozen people showed up, coming from many miles around. Some were upset about nuclear testing, that, for years had been putting radioactive Strontium-90 in babies' teeth, from the milk of cows that grazed in nuclear-contaminated fields during above-ground testing. All of us were terrified of the horrific results of a breakdown in the surreal "policy" called MAD.

All summer our group wrote letters to editors and to our elected representatives. We held demonstrations on street corners in the surrounding towns. At the county fair in August, we made a booth featuring a relief map that Merrill constructed, showing the areas circling out from New York City that would be decimated by nuclear blast and radiation. Some fair-goers called us "traitors" and "Commies," and a few angrily refused to take our leaflets, mouthing the popular Cold War slogan, *"Better Dead than Red!"* Others surreptitiously dropped money in our donations can as they hurried by—and a few brave souls even joined our SANE chapter.

My old Remington was getting a workout, as I bent over it for hours after the kids were in bed, writing letters, contacting allies, making fliers—activities that helped me feel more hopeful, and much less anxious, along with the moral support our group work provided.

Warren paid a rare solo visit to our house one afternoon in mid-summer, while Merrill was still at work and the kids were playing in our grassy fenced yard. He had been doubtful about our group activism, both of its usefulness and its ideological flavor. We sat in our small living room, which was snug and colorful with warm yellow walls, deep blue curtains and a braided Ukrainian rug. One of Merrill's tall, wraith-like wood sculptures stood in a corner, protected from accidental kiddie onslaughts by the orange butterfly chair in front of it. I brought my unexpected guest a cup of coffee and some homemade oatmeal cookies.

"Umm, thanks, these are very good. So, what is your subversive little group up to now?"

I told him about an imminent mass demonstration in New York City to demand a nuclear test-ban treaty.

"Merrill has made some great posters. We're taking the kids, of course. They say there'll be thousands marching along Third Avenue."

He sipped his coffee, fingering the pink top of his head, which still had an aureole of white hair.

"I admire your guts, my dear, but I'm very afraid that you and your friends are being used as pawns by the Soviets. This is just the sort of thing they want the intelligentsia of this country to do, to undermine our defenses!"

I protested, "All I want is to save my babies! I'm nobody's *pawn!*"

"Yes, I understand, you want to protect your children. But at the cost of their freedom?"

"What *freedom,* when everybody and everything is burnt to a crisp?"

"Your feelings are understandable." He lowered his head,

as he confessed his own sense of impotence. "It's a dilemma that I see no way out of. But I truly believe *you're playing right into Khrushchev's hands!*"

The march in New York had been exhilarating. Our group members got an emotional lift, especially when President Kennedy indicated he was willing to sign a test-ban treaty.

But in mid-October, the president announced to the nation that Soviet missiles had been installed in Cuba, and more Soviet ships were on their way. Kennedy's voice on the radio sounded grim and determined as he said that America would not stand by and let that happen; nuclear weapons only ninety miles off our shores was unacceptable. A military blockade was to be established 500 miles from the island. If Khrushchev did not turn his ships around, we would bomb them before they reached Cuba.

The Soviet leader responded that the weapons were "defensive," meant to counter American missile silos in Turkey. An attack on Russian ships would lead to war. According to the news reports, he also sounded grim and determined.

In the following days, as the missile-laden ships drew nearer to Cuba, I kept the radio on around the clock, nursing Benjy, cooking meals and carrying out the daily chores, accompanied by terrifying bulletins from first one powerful leader and then the other. Merrill went to work every day, partially, I think, needing a break from the constant barrage of bad news. Commentators speculated about which side would back down first, as if it were a street brawl. Only the few that we trusted—Walter Lippman and Edward R. Murrow among them—warned people to prepare as best they could for a nuclear war.

Warren began to drop in every day, his face purple with agitation. It was just as he had always predicted: the Russians had made their move and were preparing to take over.

Kennedy, he insisted, *must not budge*, whatever the consequences.

I realized that arguing with him increased his frenzy. I sat
quietly across the living room from him with the baby on my
lap or tried to work at some mending. One afternoon, Camilla
phoned to see if he was there. She sounded angry at me for the
first time in our acquaintance. She asked me to not to "encourage" him to make the stressful drive over the mountain.

"He's frantic; I've never seen him like this—he's going to
have a stroke or a heart attack!"

"We're *not* encouraging him, Camilla! I think he needs to
talk about it. We're all upset. I—*I'm terrified.*" I began to weep.

Camilla's voice softened. "Of course, you are, dear child.
Forgive me for ranting at you. I'm so worried about *him*, I
wasn't even thinking about you and the children."

"Camilla, our SANE group has contributed money to send
me to Washington tomorrow. They say the ships will reach the
blockade sometime tomorrow evening, and peace groups are
coming from everywhere to picket the White House. We'll
demand that Kennedy consider Khrushchev's offer to withdraw, if we take our missiles out of Turkey."

"What a brave woman you are! If it were me, I'd be too
afraid to leave my family at such a time—but, I'm sure that's
what you would prefer, too."

"Yes," I murmured. "I surely would."

On the train, I tried to read *Catch-22*, but nothing would
stick in my mind. I changed trains at Penn Station, and arriving
in the Capitol, took a cab to Pennsylvania Avenue.

The day was sunny and cool. Thousands of men and
women, all with sober, worried faces, paced back and forth
along the high black iron fence surrounding the manicured
lawns of the presidential mansion. Large numbers of somber-
looking Quakers stood silently, holding hands in a long line

facing the traffic that crept by on the broad thoroughfare. I saw posters from the Fellowship of Reconciliation, the Women's International League for Peace and Freedom, Catholic peace organizations, SANE and other anti-nuclear groups from many states. There was some comfort in the company of all these good people, who were as concerned as I was.

Bits of news and rumor trickled back to the street as small delegations met with their congressmen. We heard that the President was closeted with a top-level group of advisers, including his brother Robert, the Attorney General. It was said that the U.S. Air Force was poised to attack Cuba with thousands of bombers—that some of the generals *actually wanted to employ nuclear weapons in Cuba!*

Someone reported that Khrushchev had sent an offer to withdraw if the U.S. would agree not to attack Cuba—but this was being seen as a ploy to buy time for Russia to make their missiles operational.

Around three o'clock, a small group of us went to the office of our senator, a thoughtful man who received us kindly, but could give no comfort.

"I've been informed that SAC (Strategic Air Command) bombers are revving up on the airfield in Key West." His voice was hoarse and weary from so many days of continual crisis. "We hope Khrushchev will back down—but I can't in good conscience, advise the President to do so."

"But why not, Senator?" Urgency overcame my awe of this distinguished man, who, in the light of the apocalypse, seemed to feel as powerless as I.

"You could *go to him*, urge him to wait—*negotiate*. The Russians, and the Cubans are human, too—they don't want their children to be vaporized any more than we do. Once war starts, it'll be too late!"

"I agree with you, but the decision is up to the President now. There's nothing I can do."

In late afternoon, word came that Cuban troops were firing on U.S. reconnaissance planes, and that an American U-2 spy plane had been shot down! The fragile hopes our peaceful delegations had clung to were now changing into bleak resignation. At dark, most people dispersed, anxious to be with their families. Only the Quakers remained, keeping silent witness through the terrible night.

I made my way back to New York and to the midtown apartment of our old friends, Della and Ed Martin—wishing that I were at home, instead. The Martins gave me an excellent dinner that I could barely taste. Della, a Black woman in her thirties, was trained as an electrical engineer at a time when no such jobs were available for a woman—and a minority, at that. She was a fantastic cook, whose small gourmet dinner parties were legend, at least to those of us who sometimes got invited.

Ed was white, a superb painter of abstract art, and, like most artists we knew, held another full-time job to support his family, which now included an adorable four-year old boy, Paolo. Somehow, despite the rarity of mixed-race couples, even in New York City, at that time, these two remarkable people had brought off their complicated union and were devoted to one another.

Della had made up a comfortable cot for me in their living room. She'd sewn slipcovers and curtains out of white percale sheets, and the only bright color in the room was in Ed's paintings, one on each white wall. The effect was peaceful, like a well-ordered gallery in a museum, but warmer.

Ed and Della were soothing, too, kind and thoughtful as always. They went about their normal routines, even though they had been following the news and were eager to hear my report of the day's events.

After dinner, Ed put his son to bed, and went, as usual, into his attic studio to paint for a few hours. I tried to help Della clean up in the kitchen, but my hands were shaking and I dropped a cup I was drying.

"Oh, no! I'm so sorry, Della!"

"Don't worry about it, girl!" she said in a high singing tone. "Sit down here and relax—you've done enough today."

I dropped into a chair at the kitchen table.

"I don't understand how you guys can be so calm! I've been so terrified—for weeks now—and tonight—right now--there might be missiles blowing everything up, all around us!"

Della took two clean cups from the drainer and filled them from a steaming kettle. She shook her head with a weary smile, and sat down, pushing a cup of mint tea toward me.

"Well, if they come, *we're* not going to know about it—not for more than a second, anyway. And there's not a damned thing we can do about it. I'm not like *you*, Jan—*I* don't think I can move mountains and crusty old male politicians."

"I do feel like a fool sometimes. Right now, I just wish I'd stayed home with Merrill and the kids and left it all up to the maniacs who're in charge of everything. But I just couldn't."

Della put her hand over mine. "Well, I think you're nuts, honey, but I love you. And I wish I had your guts."

I called Merrill and asked him to put each of the children on the phone, even Ben, who managed a gurgle for his Mama.

After the Martins went to bed, I sat in the dark kitchen staring out at the lights and darks of midtown, unable to stop images of flaming skyscrapers crashing into one another. But when I finally crawled into my cot, I fell into a deep sleep, exhausted by the long, awful day.

Della woke me at six to catch my train. To my great relief, Manhattan was still there!

————

They were waiting in our old patched-up wood station wagon. As the train pulled into Sussex Station, Merrill got out of the car, carrying Benjy, bundled into his thrice-used baby-blue snowsuit. Rachel and Davy bounced out after them, running to the platform where they waved and shouted as I stepped from the train.

Rachel called, "Mama, Mama," running to me as fast as she could in her coat and thick tights; she hugged my knees, shouting, *"There's not a war, Mama, you don't have to go away anymore!"*

I dropped my things and kneeled to hug my little girl, freeing one of my arms to catch Davy as he joined us. Merrill was looking down on his huddled family with a huge grin.

"Oh, Merrill, what is it? Have you heard something?"

"Yeah, Rachel's got it right—it's on the radio this morning— Khrushchev pulled back! He made a speech on Radio Moscow. They've turned their ships around and agreed to dismantle the missiles!"

"Oh, thank God!" I wished for a moment that I believed in that fatherly deity, who could make things right with a flick of an eye. "Did they stop the bombers? We're not invading Cuba?"

"No, honey—it's all over!"

He sat down beside me on the splintery wooden platform, holding Ben so that I could kiss every one of their dear faces. The little guy gurgled and waved his arms, delighted to be at the center of such a happy riot.

By that evening, the crisis was indeed over, so far as the public was concerned. Khrushchev had capitulated. John Kennedy was a great hero, who had made the Russian bear back down. For the time being, anyway, World War III had been averted. U Thant, the Secretary General of the United Nations, would head a delegation to monitor the removal of Cuban missile sites.

In reality, of course, the powerful war machine was not so easy to stop. General Curtis Lemay, chief of the air force, wanted to go ahead and bomb the hell out of Cuba, while Fidel Castro thundered, *"Khrushchev has no cojones!"*

Much later, Americans learned that Kennedy had agreed to withdraw Jupiter missiles from Turkey, and to stop preparations for war on Cuba—to the fury of hard-line anticommunists.

Most Americans let out a huge sigh of relief and told themselves, "Thank heaven that's over!" But some people could not go on as before. Warren had a mental breakdown and had to be hospitalized. Camilla told me that he was still wildly agitated, after several weeks, and was convinced that Communists were trying to kill him. He refused medication, and she didn't know how she was going to manage.

Merrill and I felt that the call had been too close. We knew the next crisis could come at any time, and that northeastern New Jersey would still be one of the most vulnerable places on the planet. We made a firm decision to move our family to California, where Merrill had grown up and where his mother and five scattered siblings lived.

I made up my mind that, for my own mental health, I would have to find a job that used my education and other strengths that had gone slack during my baby-bearing years.

I told Merrill, "Maybe I can make enough money so you can stay home with the kids and do sculpture!"

He guffawed.

"Oh, you bet, I'll have a lot of time for sculpture while I'm dealing with these monkeys. . . but it sure would be wonderful if we could pull it off!" His eyes sparkled— "I've been thinking about Sausalito—you'd love it, honey, it's on this gorgeous hillside looking over the Bay, across from San Francisco. A lot of artists live there, in houseboats. . . maybe we could . . ."

He couldn't sit still. He got out of bed, naked, and paced around the bedroom, warm with excitement on the chilly November night.

"I would love that," I said, meaning it—but inside me, a sense of desolation persisted.

"They must have a lot of anti-nuclear groups out there. I'll join something."

"Sure! Hey, let's leave in time to visit your folks in Florida for Christmas. . . I wish we could go tomorrow!"

"Me too, babe, but get back in here before you catch your death!"

He slid in beside me and pulled the blankets over us both, holding me close. As he sought my mouth and began to move tenderly over me, I took a measure of hope from his glowing optimism. But I doubted that I would ever feel safe again.

My Murderers

Going to Jail—Part 1

"Oh, geez—this is really weird!" I moaned to Sam, my almost new husband, who was driving me to the North Bay Women's Correctional Facility (i.e., jail) near the eastern edge of Silicon Valley.

"I know *all* the guards, and a lot of inmates—not to mention Lieutenant Bramley! She'll have me right where she wants me now!"

Sam's calm grey eyes left the road briefly to glance at my anxious face, which I hadn't bothered to make up this morning. The guards would make me scrub myself in the de-licing shower as soon as I checked in, and I'd have to change from my own soft blue jeans into the stiff jail version.

"She probably won't even notice you're there, honey. It's only twenty-four hours."

I slumped down; the seatbelt rode up painfully on my lower ribs.

"I *wish. She'll* notice—nothing gets past that woman.

Anyway, what d'you *mean, only* twenty-four hours? Have you ever tried to sleep in a bunk bed, in a room with fifty other people, with one eye open? Half of these women are drug addicts or have some other kind of mental problem!"

"Hey, babe, don't forget, I spent three years in the Army."

I propped my knees against the glove compartment and wrapped my arms around them.

"It's not the same," I mumbled.

He slipped his right hand under my ponytail and softly massaged the back of my neck.

My antinuclear group and I had practiced going limp while being dragged off to police vehicles—paddy wagons, patrol cars, buses; we were advised to take candy bars, water bottles, and plastic bags to pee in, in case we were held for hours without such amenities. We learned to tense up our wrists while the handcuffs were being cinched, so that they'd be looser, maybe even slip-outable, when we relaxed them.

We had looked forward to getting arrested for trespassing, when we would step over the forbidden boundary of a sprawling missile-assembly plant. We'd hand informational leaflets to the workers—innocent pawns who toted their lunch pails through the guarded iron gates every morning, probably proud to think they were helping defend their country. There they would assemble components of missiles that were intended to slaughter hundreds of thousands of other blameless men, women and children—in one blip on a radar screen—by one push of a lever!

After all that preparation, the protest had been anticlimactic—there was no violence on either side. Our group of thirty women and men, aged seventeen to eighty-two, arrived very early, and distributed a few hundred leaflets before a dozen police officers approached us in phalanx, at a run, just as we stepped over a thick iron chain marked with bright yellow "*DO NOT CROSS—DANGER RADIATION*" signs.

An officer read us our rights, we were duly handcuffed by freshman cops (kids who seemed more scared of us than we of them). We were led one-by-one to a waiting bus, and thence to a police station where we were booked, photographed, finger-printed, quickly arraigned by a judge, and charged with tres-passing (a misdemeanor.)

All pled *nolo contendere*—that is, we acknowledged that, although they had us for crossing the line, we denied that we were guilty of anything, since in our view, we were trying to *save the whole damned human race from nuclear war!*

Most of my fellow lawbreakers stayed to serve their time—twenty-four hours—then and there—but because I had kids to arrange care for, and clients to see, I took the option of serving my sentence a couple of weeks later. In a few days, I'd get a notice telling me which facility I would turn myself into.

It wasn't until I received that notice, that it finally dawned on me that *I'd be locked up in the same jail where I'd served for the past two years as a counselor!*

"Poor little girl." Sam's voice was gentle, his hand warm on my neck, and for a moment I relaxed. Then he added, in a more matter-of-fact tone, "You *did* ask for it, you know."

I sat upright, pushing his hand away. "I wanted to stand up for *peace*—to protest against *nuclear Armageddon!* There are plenty of other jails they could have sent me to—how could I know I'd end up *here?*"

A few years before, this area had been apricot and cherry orchards, or lettuce and strawberry fields, but now every few hundred yards there was a vast new complex of buildings, elec-tronic start-ups that were suddenly hugely successful and able to afford spiffy designs and landscaping.

We drove by pastures where a few cows grazed. An occasional small, white heron was perched on a rail fence or on a cow's stoic back. When I worked out here, I'd always enjoyed this part of the commute; I'd slow down to savor my last few minutes of freedom before entering the jail compound, hoping to spot one of the screaming peacocks that some fanciful person had once donated to the facility.

The jail consisted of two long, flat buildings, built in ghastly grey cement rectangles; the larger of them was the men's minimum-security jail, where non-violent offenders did their time working in the fields that backed up to the structures. But the women here were all locked in, with nothing to do and no sight or sound of fields and birds and sky—sometimes for a year or more, in the case of those waiting for trial.

Today, I had to be there by seven to turn myself in. I patted Sam's knee.

"Oh, Sam. You're absolutely right, of course. It's only twenty-four hours. So many women have to stay in there for months and months!"

He covered my hand with his own. "It'll be over before you know it."

"Yeah. Right! Just be sure you're back here tomorrow at seven sharp!"

Jilli

Two years earlier

"Hey, psych-lady! I wanna talk to you."

Jilli leaned against the front of her cell, her long, perfect, blood-red fingernails gripping the iron door.

"Okay, sure. How about right after lunch?"

"That's mail-call. I'm s'posed to get some money from my mom today. What about after that?"

"Nothing till four."

"Okay, *I'll be here!*"

Funny joke. The women in the felony section at the back half of the too-small one-story building, were only allowed out of their cells for thirty minutes a day to go into the dank "exercise yard." This was a narrow pen about 20 x 30 feet, with concrete-block walls two stories high, topped by coils of razor wire, and containing a netless basketball hoop. Their only other respite from their crowded cells, except for meals, was when they came to me for "therapy," which usually meant that they liked to sit and gab for half an hour on the big flowered cushions on the floor of my office.

A deputy would accompany me to the inmate's cell and escort the prisoner back to my hole-in-the-wall, a converted bathroom, six feet by eleven, with my desk where the toilet had recently stood.

With a small budget for decorating, I'd put a bright yellow shag rug on the floor and pictures of flowers and scenery on the walls, but no chairs—they took up too much space. With cushions, we could sit with our backs against the beige walls, pull our knees up or sit cross-legged facing each other. The intimacy helped encourage the women to talk—that plus the fact that, as my supervisor said when she showed me around on my first day, "Don't worry, they'll talk to you. You'll be the only nice person here."

At that point, I'd worked at the jail for about three weeks, still trying to get used to the morning routine: being identified through a tiny, thick glass window, buzzed in by a uniformed, female guard, who would open the first of two massive, metal doors. I'd be let into an anteroom where the deputies locked up their guns (they couldn't take them into the jail proper, where they could be lifted by some of the light-fingered clientele), then escorted through the second door. Each door slammed behind one with a clanging crash, which confirmed, in case you hadn't noticed, that you were now quite securely locked in.

As soon as I got inside that morning, Brenda, one of the deputies, called out to me from the bullpen, an open office area, in the center of the jail, "Hey, Jan! The lieutenant wants you to check out the 187 in number fourteen."

"Okay. What's a 187?" Brenda's face showed no expression as she continued her two-fingered typing.

"Murder," she said in a flat tone, without looking up.

I unlocked the door to my office, into which they'd cut a small hole for a window, since otherwise the room would've been unbearably claustrophobic. Also, it was a safety feature for me, in case a customer decided to cut my throat with a sharpened spoon. (I presumed, and hoped, that the guards glanced in there once in a while as they made their rounds.)

I stowed my purse and jacket in the big drawer at the bottom of my desk, and tried to get a handle on the idea of going into a small, locked cell with a "187."

While some version of "therapy" took place in my office, the first interview usually happened in the inmate's cell, sometimes by request of the prisoner and sometimes, as in this case, when the deputies wanted an assessment of the woman's mental status. Was she too psychotic or violent to be housed in a two-woman cell, or would she have to be placed in an isolation unit, with pads on the walls, no toilet or bunk, just a drain hole in the concrete floor? After twelve years as a therapist in a county mental health clinic, I'd seen and treated most everything, from wildly manic psychotics and child molesters to drug dealers, but this was something different. I was excited and a little scared.

I didn't dare let myself take much time to think about it. I was the first professional counselor they'd hired at the jail (not counting a psychiatrist who came once a week to assess the need for and to dispense psychoactive medication). It was clear that I, personally, as well as the concept of an in-house shrink itself, were still very much on probation. The deputies, all of whom were women, and the uptight lieutenant in charge, Christine Bramley—were extremely dubious about my being there at all. They'd let me know from the first that they expected me to get in their way, that my services were a kind of frill, an unnecessary and demoralizing coddling of offenders, and that, in any case, a sappy do-gooder like me would never be able to take the guff from the hard-bitten bitches who came back again and again on prostitution, drug, battery and larceny charges.

As a mental health professional, I felt obligated, not only to do some good for these hapless women, if possible, but to set a precedent for the future of mental health in the jails, which, I had no doubt, needed it more than almost anywhere else.

But no one had mentioned murderers! When I took this job, I hadn't even considered that, in the county jail, there might sometimes *be* murderers—or at least, people so accused.

I imagined Brenda and one of her pals, giving each other sardonic smiles as they watched me head back toward the felony cells, trying hard to look calm and professional. The deputies wouldn't want me to get hurt, I reassured myself—*that* wouldn't look good for *them*. The "187" must be harmless—now. Anyway, prisoners are innocent until proven guilty, aren't they? I'd always believed that, but in the jail, the assumption was that anybody who was there had got there for good reasons, and I realized I'd already picked up some of that attitude. (*The innocence of the knee-jerk liberal going right out the window, when smack up against a different reality.*)

Marta, a tall, muscular blond deputy who had never before spoken a word to me, and who never, as far as I could tell, smiled in the course of her day's work, opened number fourteen for me and told me tersely that the prisoner's name was Jilli Briggs. I took a quick look inside the cell, where a small woman of about thirty, bleached platinum hair still damp from the de-licing shower, sat on the edge of an iron cot, doubled over, head in her hands, rocking back and forth. Her bare arms, marked with home-made hearts-with-arrows tattoos, looked cold and skinny in the white jail-issue T-shirt with "*Property of North Bay Women's Correctional Facility*" stenciled on the back in red.

She didn't *look* very menacing, I thought, just profoundly miserable, as new prisoners generally did. Still, you couldn't be sure. Maybe I should ask Marta to stay near the cell while I was in there, just to be safe. But that would just prove what a wimp I was.

I stepped inside the brightly lighted cell. "Thanks," I told Marta. She locked the door behind me and lumbered away down the wide aisle between the two rows of felony cells.

"Hi, Jilli?" I said quietly. The woman lifted her head slightly, and squinted at me through wet, swollen eyes, surprised, I guessed, by the sound of a gentle voice in that place. Then she hid her face again and went on rocking.

I told her my name, explaining that I was a mental health

counselor, not a cop, and anything she said to me would be just between us.

"Yeah, right," she muttered into her long-fingered, bony hands. That day her nails were bitten halfway down to the cuticles, and some of them were rimmed with blackish-red dried blood—from her own savage gnawing of them, I thought.

I sat down a few feet away on the rough, tightly tucked-in wool blanket that covered the bunk.

"How'd you happen to end up here?"

"I didn't do *nothin'*." An indistinct mumble through her lank hair and the tortured hands. Then she looked up at me with weary indignation in her thin, almost- pretty face. "The fuckin' cops came to my house at two A.M. in the morning and dragged me in here—all's I had on was my nightie!"

"How terrible! You must've been so scared. What did they tell you?"

"A shitful of *lies*! *They said I shot somebody-and they're* dead. *I didn't kill nobody*! I don't even know *who it is* I'm s'posed to've killed!"

"That sounds awful! Why do they think that?"

By now, Jilli's anger had supplanted her despair and she tried to clean up her dripping nose and red eyes with the miserably inadequate wipes the County supplied. She blew her nose on four or five of them, one after the other, tossing each crumpled tissue on the floor.

"Beats the shit outa me," she railed. "The fuckin' neighbors were partyin' all night long, a lot of people yellin' and playin' their fuckin' music so loud nobody could sleep in the whole neighborhood!"

"Boy, that can drive you nuts."

"You're fuckin' right! *Somebody* had to *do* somethin'—no use callin' the cops, they never come when you *need* 'em. My husband went out back and yelled at those people to shut the fuck up about fifty times, but they never paid no attention. So finally, Jimmy, he got his rifle and shot it a couple times up in the air—just some warnin' shots to get their attention."

"Did that work?"

"No fuckin' way! You could hear 'em laughin' like it was all a big fuckin' joke. So then *I* got Jimmy's .38 and his .45 and went out there and screamed at 'em, and then *I* took a few shots in the air, too."

Jilli dropped her head into her hands again, and I thought she might be too upset to continue just then, but when I asked her, she jerked her small head in a decided negative, and went on in an almost wondering tone:

"Then, like, all of a sudden, people started screamin' and they were yellin' all, 'Call 9-1-1,' and first thing I know, about a million sirens come down our street, ambulances and the pigs and the fire department-- I don't know who all, and then these cops came pounding' on our door and they dragged me and Jimmy out and threw us in a cop car."

"They told you somebody next door got killed?"

She groaned. "Yeah, I guess. Some *woman*." Her small, greenish eyes were dry now, wide with dull amazement as she stared into mine. "But it *could'na* been *me* that shot her. Or Jimmy. We only fired in the air. We never shot at nobody. No way it coulda been us!"

I would have liked to ask her a lot more questions, such as, why did they have all those guns, and was she sure she didn't make just one little slip and fire too low, and had they had trouble with those neighbors before last night? But I caught myself in time. Any of them would have sounded to her like cop-questions and turned her off for good.

"What do *you* think happened, Jilli?"

"*Shit*, I don't know, man. I guess a bullet coulda --whatcha-call-it—*ricocheted* off somethin' and hit that woman."

She looked stunned for a minute, as if she'd just realized that in fact, somebody had died, and that she might have had something to do with it. Then she set her pointed little jaw and said with dark suspicion, "Unless one of those people *over there* did it, and they're just usin' Jimmy and me as a cover. I wouldn't put it past that bunch!"

"I guess the police can check that out, with, uh, ballistic testing?"

"Yeah, I guess."

"What a tough break. You must feel terrible." I put my hand softly on her shoulder and bent to look into her face.

"Jilli, I have to ask: at this point, are you having any feelings like you might want to hurt yourself—or somebody else?"

"*Hurt* myself? Shit, *no*, I just wanta get the hell outa here! First, I gotta find out what happened to Jimmy. I never hurt *nobody*, never in my life!"

She turned her head away and wiped her reddened eyes with the heel of her hand, adding, "The only reason I got a little record for assault-and-battery is behind that dumb bitch that came onto Jimmy a couple years ago at a club. But then I was drinkin'. I don't drink no more. Nothin' but beer."

I told Jilli I'd be here every weekday, and if she wanted to come to my office and talk, she just had to ask a deputy, or snag me as I walked by.

"I ain't gonna be here that long," she said with determination.

"I hope you're right, but I'll be here if you want to talk."

I called out to Marta, who was standing nearby in the corridor, and she came to let me out. Then I headed past the misdemeanor dorm and down a narrow hallway, crowded with stacks of cardboard boxes, to the lieutenant's office.

I tapped on the door, which was slightly ajar, and Lt. Bramley motioned me inside. She was on the phone, frowning, impatient, trying to keep her temper and maintain a gracious tone in spite of her clenched jaw. She kept her ice-blue eyes focused on her heaped desk blotter as she talked.

"Yes, certainly, I understand completely, and I want to assure your committee that we're doing absolutely everything we can to resolve the overcrowding problem. . . *Yes*, you bet, the Sheriff's Department is fully aware of the situation. . . .Umm— Well, of course, your delegation is welcome to tour the jail any time. Just let me know when you want to come."

Lt. Bramley had wrapped a wide swath of her fiery red hair around a small, balled fist, and l was concerned that she was on the verge of pulling it right out of her scalp.

"No, of course not, I assure you, we're very grateful for your concern. It keeps us on our toes. Okay, goodbye, now."

She put the phone down with exaggerated care, glared up at me, and exploded.

"Why the *hell* don't these people with nothing to do but meddle *leave me alone*! I've got a jail to run here. I'm so backed up I'll never catch up, and these do-gooders want to come in here every five minutes and 'inspect' the place—as if they have any idea what it takes to control a pack of ninety-plus animals and keep three dozen deputies happy with their schedules and their powder-room facilities and . . ." She stopped and took a deep breath, perhaps remembering that she was talking to somebody she didn't trust, and who was very likely on *the other side*. The soft-on-criminals side—maybe even, a *spy*.

"Okay, Ms. Harwood. What is it?"

"You wanted an assessment of Jilli Briggs?"

"Who? Oh, yeah, the new 187. What do you think?"

"She's calm, lucid, not a danger to herself or others. She can be housed in a regular cell."

"Okay. Thanks. She give you any idea why she killed that woman?"

"Sorry, Lieutenant, I can't comment on anything like that. You know."

I wished I could tell her that I believed it was an accident, that Jilli had been careless—to say the least! but probably hadn't meant to kill anybody—but if I started doing that, patient confidentiality would be meaningless, the police would begin to expect me to be a shill, to find out and report the prisoners' secrets. The lieutenant abruptly dismissed me by turning back to her telephone. She swivelled her chair around to face the dark-green file cabinets that lined the back of the room.

———

Two months had passed since that day, and I was beginning to feel like an old-timer, a hard case, myself, locked in every day from eight to five, except for my blessed lunch hour. When I heard those doors slam behind me every morning, I felt like I just might never get out.

I had expected Jilli to make bail right away, but the State was trying to prove that she had a motive to kill her neighbor, that there was bad blood between the two households before the shooting, that she'd taken careful aim when she shot that .45. Her previous conviction for a violent act hadn't helped her lawyer get the dismissal he was seeking, and her bail was set too high for her family to make.

Jilli came to my office a couple of times a week. Her bitten nails had time to grow out and be wrapped by a volunteer manicurist who came in every Tuesday.

Many of the women used their jail time to rest and get clean from their various addictions, as well as to learn a lot of new techniques, tricks and dodges from their cohorts. With no work to do, they lay around with their hair uncombed, their thighs and paunches swelling on the jail diet of three big, fat-

and-cholesterol- laden meals a day—but most of them sported long, sleek, gleaming fingernails.

At first, Jilli was frantic and enraged that they were charging her with murder. But after she found out that Jimmy had been allowed to go home, and she could talk to him once a day on the phone, she'd settled into a fairly comfortable routine, learning to crochet—and God knows what else—from her cell-mate, a recidivist thief who stole to support her own and her boyfriend's drug habits. Most of the women crocheted; they could buy yarn at the once-a-week commissary. Many cells were bright with afghans in pink, orange, green, purple.

I was convinced that Jilli was innocent of any intent to kill. The more I got to know her, the more I saw her as a perfectly ordinary, not-too-bright girl who'd dropped out of high school to get married, stayed close to her family, worked off and on as a waitress, and sampled a bit of whatever drugs came her way— but had never got seriously addicted to anything. I'd tried to probe a little into her childhood, see if I could dig up any serious neuroses, to make our sessions more useful for her—and interesting for me; but, after a while it was clear that, as with many of my jail clients, all she wanted—or needed—from me, was a friendly sounding board for her current frustrations and anxieties.

Consuela

I still hadn't been able to interview Consuela, although she'd been brought in three nights before, according to the deputies, raving mad, screaming, talking wild gibberish. Every time I went to her cell, she was just a lump of blanket, facing the wall, knees curled under her chin, and when I tried to get her to talk, she rolled over and went back to sleep.

I asked the deputies to tell me if she got any visitors, and Brenda came and got me when Consuela's sister, Ana, arrived on Thursday morning.

"Thanks, Brenda. And I'd appreciate it if you'd wait a few minutes before you bring Consuela in, so I'll have some time with her sister." Brenda chuckled without mirth.

"She hasn't been up yet except to pee and eat. Her sister's probably out of luck."

I crossed a dozen yards of mottled vinyl flooring in the bleak visitors' area, where a small woman sat in one of a row of molded-plastic chairs. She held a shiny black purse in her lap. With her black-jacketed arms wrapped around her chest, and her thin legs tucked back under the chair seat, she seemed to be trying to sink into the wall. There were half a dozen other visitors in the room who sat with their backs to Ana and me, already talking to their wives, daughters, sisters or girlfriends on phones that conducted their voices through a thick glass wall.

"Hello—Ana Perez?"

She barely lifted her eyes, saw I wasn't in police uniform, and nodded slightly. Ana was a few years younger and considerably thinner than her sister, Consuela, but she appeared worn out and unkempt; her limp black hair looked as though it hadn't been washed for a while, and there were dark smudges under her tired brown eyes. I wasn't surprised, since I knew from the deputies' reports that she'd been through hell in the past few days. Her house had burned down in the middle of the night, she, her husband and two small children had barely escaped with their lives, and their seventy-year-old mother—hers and Consuela's, had died in the fire. Consuela had been charged with first-degree homicide.

I took a chair next to Ana's.

"I'm Mrs. Harwood, the mental health counselor here. I know you're going through a very painful time. I'm so sorry."

She continued to stare down at the shiny, patent-leather purse in her lap.

"We'd like to help Consuela, but we don't have any background on her mental health history. I was hoping you could fill me in."

She muttered something I couldn't quite make out.

"Excuse me? I couldn't hear you."

Ana lifted her head then and her eyes, full of hopelessness and anger, focused on my face.

"We don't want no counselors! It's too late. She already did it. Anyway, nobody can help Consuela, she's crazy, ever since she was a kid. They had her in the hospital till last March and then they said she was okay. She had no place to go, so we took her in. And *now* look what happened."

"It was a terrible thing." I paused, and then went on. "I haven't had a chance to talk to your sister yet. Our doctor put her on some strong tranquilizers when she first came in, and she sleeps most of the time. Do you have any idea why she set the fire?"

Ana popped open the brass clasp of her purse and then shut it again with a sharp snap.

"Because she's crazy! Why does Consuela do anything? She's crazy, like always, they should never have let her out of that state hospital! Before, they said she'd be there for all her life, and then they told us she was okay and could go home with us."

Ana was becoming more agitated by the moment, snapping and unsnapping her purse. I spoke quietly.

"Yes, she's a very sick woman. Did she have some medication to take?"

"Sure, she had a sackful of bottles, some kinda pills, I don't know what all kinds she had. At first it made her sleep a lot at my house, and that was good, she didn't bother nobody all day, but then last week she stayed up all night, going down to the kitchen, opened the doors to our bedrooms, just stood there looking at us in our beds. My husband yelled at her to go back to bed and she did. But that night . . ."

Ana's face had grown flushed, and her eyes red with held-back tears. She took a fistful of pink tissues from her purse.

"Did she stop taking her pills?"

"I think that's what happened. I told her every morning, did you take your pills, Consuela?, and she just smiled and nodded at me like always. She was always smiling, happy like a little girl. She wouldn't hurt nobody if she wasn't crazy. Consuela was not normal, not since she was a kid, but she never *hurt* nobody." Tears poured down her sallow cheeks now, and she sobbed into her tissues.

I laid my hand gently on her shoulder. "I'm so sorry, Ana. You've been through so much. I'm very sorry about your mother."

Ana spoke through her tears. "Mama loved Consuela *so much*. She always said *she* couldn't help it if she was sick—forty-one years old and she was still Mama's *nina*. But she was mad that Mama wouldn't let her come in her room--she'd pull things out of the drawers and mess up Mama's lipstick and stuff, so she made Consuela stay outside her room. Maybe that's why she made the fire. *But she wouldn't hurt Mama if she knew. She didn't know what she was doing!*"

"Had she ever set a fire before?"

Ana pushed a strand of lank hair back from her face and nodded. "She used to play with matches, Mama'd slap her hand and tell her no, and we'd hide the matches ... but one time, she was about thirteen, she got ahold of one and made a fire in the kitchen. That's the first time they put her in the hospital."

"It's nice that you came to see her."

"Mama would want me to visit her. Mama always went to see her at the hospital, every week. I *know* she can't help being sick. I don't want her to get the gas chamber or whatever, for what she done."

I stood up. "Thank you so much for talking to me, Ana. We'll do whatever we can to help her. I'll ask the deputy to bring her to the window now, if she's awake, so you two can talk."

"Okay, thank you, Mrs." Ana looked up at me with the smallest hint of hope and gratitude in her lightless eyes.

The deputy hadn't been able to rouse Consuela, even when she was told her sister was here to visit.

"I'll go tell the lady she might as well go home."

"Thanks, Brenda."

I asked Dr. Hamill to consider reducing Consuela's dose of Thorazine and I called around to search for her old medical records. If she'd been treated at the county mental health clinics, there'd be a case history we could look at. It wasn't so easy to get the old state hospital records, with so many closed.

A few days later, I tried again to talk to Consuela. From her record, which a caseworker had summed up for me over the phone, her diagnosis was paranoid schizophrenia, with an IQ of 52. The doctor had reduced her dose of psychotropic drugs, and after several days, a deputy reported that she was staying awake for a few hours each day. She had no cellmate, despite the crowded conditions, since nobody knew how she might react to another person in the tight space.

I found her sitting on the edge of the lower bunk, fully dressed in oversized jeans and grey sweatshirt and sneakers. She was turning the pages of a comic book.

"Hi, Consuela. D'you remember me? I'm the counselor, Jan Harwood. I've come to see you several times before, but you were always too sleepy to talk to me."

"Hi." She smiled brightly, her face round and tan, small nose and black eyes nearly lost in her chubby cheeks.

"Consuela, do you know where you are? What this place is?"

"Yeah, it's jail," she said, continuing to beam up at me. "It's a jail, right?"

I sat down a few feet away from her on the bunk. "Yes, it's the North Bay Womens' Correctional Facility—the women's jail. How are you feeling?"

"Okay!" *Quite perky in fact*, I thought.

"Consuela, do you know why you're here?"

She turned a page in her comic book and held it up an inch from my eyes.

"Look, Spiderman! He's my best favorite, Spiderman."

I took her pudgy, outstretched hand and moved the comic book back several inches.

"Ah, yes, I see him. He's one of my favorites, too. Maybe we can read it together some time. But, for now, could you put the book down now and talk to me a little bit?"

"Okay," she grinned, and turning her thick torso, put the comic behind her on the bunk, covered it with her pillow and gave it a gentle pat.

"I can't read, but I like the pictures. Spiderman—like a *man* that's a *spider!*"

"Thank you for putting it down for now. Okay, so why are you here, Consuela? Do you know why you're in jail?"

"They said I made a fire. I'm not supposed to make fires. Mama yells at me when I play with matches."

"That's right, there was a fire. Do you remember it?"

She looked blankly at me, her pale pink mouth slightly open. "No, but they said I made it. That's why they put me in jail for it."

"You don't remember the fire at all?"

She shook her head. Her straight, dull black hair was cut short and blunt, mental-hospital style, short bangs pasted to her damp forehead with greasy sweat. Her smile faded, became a babyish pout.

"Mama's mad at me. She don't let me come in her room and play with her things. I wish she'd come see me in jail."

Oh, God, I thought. *She doesn't know her mother died in the fire.*

I knew whose job it would be to tell her. I worried that if she got it from the deputies or a lawyer, it might be in a brusque fashion that could send her back into raving psychosis or catatonia.

"Consuela," I said very gently, "do you know that your house burned down? Ana's house?"

She nodded with her opaque wide-eyed smile.

"I played with matches. That's why they brought me in jail. I love Spiderman," she said, turning to dig her comic book from under the rumpled pillow. She hugged the book to her big, soft chest.

"It was nighttime when the house burned down. Everybody was asleep, and when they woke up, the house was on fire. Do you remember that?"

"No. It was a big fire. That's why Mama's mad."

I scooted closer and put my arm around her shoulders, which she accepted without question.

"You and Ana and Jesus and the little boys were lucky—you all got out of the house before you got hurt."

Consuela hugged and patted her book.

"Spiderman would fly in the house and save them. He wouldn't let nobody get hurt."

"But, you see, dear, your Mama *couldn't* get out."

I took a breath, and forced myself to go on.

"Honey, your Mama died in the fire."

She laid the comic book in her lap, licked a broad, dimpled finger, and began turning the bright pages, rocking, singing a little tuneless song.

"Did you understand, honey? Your mama is gone—dead."

"Spiderman, oh Spiderman, oh Spiderman," she sang softly. She smiled.

"Mama bought me this book. It's my favorite."

I stood up, feeling a bit woozy.

"Okay, Consuela. I'll see you tomorrow—or any time you want to talk to me. Just tell a deputy . . ."

She went on rocking, singing and turning pages.

A couple of weeks later, when I made my almost daily visit to her cell, I found her wide awake, dressed in an oversized cotton smock and a pair of pink plastic flip-flops.

"Hey, Consuela. How ya doin'?"

"Okay. See what I made?"

She held out a small, lopsided rectangle of Day-Glo orange crochet. In the drab cell, the scrap flared like a tiny bonfire.

"That's very pretty. What's it going to be?"

"It's a afghan for mama. She died, you know."

She pulled at the strand that connected her handiwork to a mare's nest of acrylic yarn in her lap.

"Want me to help you untangle your yarn?"

"Okay."

"When we get this straightened out, we'll roll it into a ball, so it won't get tangled again."

"Okay." Consuela gave a sudden tug at the strand, pulling the snarls I'd loosened tight again.

"Hmm." I frowned at the orange coils, considering how to sort out the much more complex tangle in her childlike mind.

"You're feeling much better now than when you first came here, aren't you, Consuela?"

"Yeah. Ana says I'm real good. I take my pills every day."

"That's great. You know, you'll be going to court tomorrow, for your trial. And I'll be there, too."

"Okay." She picked up a fat, plastic crochet hook and began scratching her scalp.

"Your lawyer, Mr. Donahue, asked me to testify—to tell the judge about how sick you were when you set the fire at Ana's house. Do you know what a trial is, Consuela?"

"Yeah, I seen it on TV. They ask you questions."

"That's right. And you tell them true answers, so the judge knows how to decide where you go."

"Can I go home tomorrow?"

"No, hon, I'm sure they won't let you go home. I hope the judge will let you go to a nice hospital."

I set down the hopeless glob of yarn and turned to look into her eyes.

"You know, honey, you started the fire, and the house burned down. The judge has to decide what your punishment is for that. And there was something a lot worse. You know, don't you, that your Mama got hurt?"

She sighed. "Ana says Mama died. That's why she didn't come see me."

"That's right," I said gently.

Consuela stood up and shuffled across the four feet to the

barred front of her cell, and then circled back to where I sat; then she made the trek all over again, stopping in front of me. She struggled to understand the incomprehensible.

"Why did Mama die? Was she sick?"

My heart felt very large and heavy in my chest. Now that she might be able to understand—at least a little bit—she needed to know the truth before she went to her trial.

"You see, dear, she didn't wake up when the fire was all around her in the house, so she breathed in too much smoke. The smoke killed her, Consuela."

Her eyes widened, tears began streaming down her cheeks. She continued to stare into my eyes through the deluge.

"My mama died—in the fire? Did I *make her die?*"

"Yes, dear. I know you didn't mean to hurt her."

I moved to put my arms out to her, but the poor woman suddenly threw herself face-down on the bunk and began beating on it with both fists. She pulled the pillow over her face, her thick body rolling back and forth, drawn into repeated, agonizing spasms.

Women in the facing cells across the wide aisle stared, trying to see what was going on. A deputy walked over and peered into the cell. I shook my head, murmured, "It's okay, she'll be all right."

Consuela howled, wordless, infant-like cries of terrible grief and pain and loss. I stood by her, helpless to undo what she had done.

As I had thought she would, the judge remanded Consuela to one of the few remaining state hospitals, where, I hoped, she and Spiderman could safely live out their strange lives.

Tina

Shrill screams and stern, authoritative shouts from the felony section. Not uncommon, when some prisoner felt unfairly treated by the staff, or had a tiff with her cellmate. But the clamor escalated, and all at once, five or six deputies left their posts in the bullpen and rushed toward the scene, billy clubs drawn, weighted down by their thick, navy pants and jackets, black belts, bunches of big brass keys, heavy boots.

I'd just returned from my lunch hour, which I'd found myself stretching out a little bit longer every day. It was salvation to get out of those grim walls for an hour—just to reassure myself that I could.

As I moved cautiously toward the racket, I saw a herd of six or seven women cops at the end of the cellblock, converging on Tina, a Black heroin addict and prostitute, who was shrieking furiously.

"*No*, fuck you, motherfuckers I ain't goin' back in there, they rats in there, big motherfuckin' rats!"

With the crazed strength of adrenaline-infused terror, she was resisting the efforts of two big deputies to shove her into the cell. Some of the cops who'd rushed into the fray had their nightsticks drawn and raised. Until then, I'd never seen any actual physical violence or bloodshed in the place, which, on the whole, ran pretty smoothly—but now some sort of mayhem seemed inevitable.

From long acquaintance with severely agitated people in my work at crisis clinics, it was obvious to me that Tina's panic was in no way assuaged by a gang of grim-faced cops coming at her. Without further thought, I somehow slipped through the pack of uniforms to the screaming woman's side and put my arm around her skinny shoulders.

"Hey, Tina, it's okay, nobody's going to hurt you, they just want you to go back into your cell, that's all, come on hon, you'll be safe there, that's all they want, come on, sweetie, I'll go in there with you, it'll be okay. . ." I urged, and, as I had been sure she would, Tina quieted down and the two of us walked peacefully into the six-by ten-foot cell. Except for ever-vigilant Marta, the deputies, thwarted but relieved, hands on hips, sheathed their nightsticks and drifted away in muttering twos and threes.

I sat with Tina on her bunk as she told me how she'd been attacked in the night by a huge rat that had come up out of the seatless toilet in her cell. She showed me a large, suppurating lesion on her upper arm that had joined an armful of old tracks —scars from previous needle infections.

"Look here, where the fucker bit me!"

"Wow, that's awful. Has the doc seen that?"

"Yeah, he give me pills, but he say it's from needles, he don't believe me about the rats, they big as a cat, come in here at night and don't nobody but me see 'em! Doc's no good anyway, he won't give me no Valium, just that fuckin' Thorazine to kick with, that stuff don't do me no good. I been hurtin' all over my damn body, like I'm gonna die in here—and then the *rats* crawlin' on me when I'm try to get some sleep."

"I'll ask the doc if you can get something that works better. Kicking in here is a hard way to go."

"You say that right." Her tense, battered body began to relax and tears streamed down her dark brown face, spotted with hard little black freckles.

"Nobody care if you dyin' all twisted up in a big knot and shakin' all over, don't matter how many blankets you got on you, nobody in this place give a shit!"

Tina had been busted for selling, and with several previous convictions behind her, would probably do hard time in prison after her trial.

I handed her the roll of toilet paper.

"Aren't you just a little bit glad to get clean, though?"

"Yeh, shit, I was strung out bad, man, cost me a couple hundred a day; I had to let my mama take the kids, I couldn't take care of 'em no more. But I'm scared o' goin' to Frontera. They say that a *real* bad place. Could you tell 'em to let me do my time in here? This place *bad*, but it ain't no fuckin' *prison*."

She pulled a five-foot length of tissue off the roll, coiled it around her hand, and mopped her face.

"I'll sure make the recommendation, but I have no control over that, you know. It's up to the judge."

"That all I'm askin', lady, jus' recommen' for me. Shit, I'm tired."

I stood up and Tina lay down on the edge of the narrow bunk, trying to pull the wool blanket out of its tight tuck to cover herself with the small strip she wasn't lying on.

"Can you get me a extra blanket?" she asked, her eyes already closed.

"Sure, that I can do."

I called for Marta, who stood eight feet away, arms folded and sturdy legs apart. She came toward us, a bit wary.

"Marta, could Tina please have an extra blanket?"

Marta looked relieved, slightly relaxing her stiff posture.

"Sure, I'll getcha one, hold on a minute." She sorted out a key from the jangling bunch on her belt and unlocked the large supply room at the far end of the cell block. In a few minutes, she was back with a blanket. I draped it over Tina, who was lying in fetal position, shaking and moaning.

Marta let me out, and, still feeling a little shaky, I went to see my next client, three cells down.

Bitsy

She was nineteen, with a short Afro that framed her heart-shaped, milk-chocolate face like a black halo. She wore her jail jeans and shirts with the grace of a model, dimpled adorably whenever she smiled, which was most of the time, and was friendly and outgoing with everyone, even Marta. Bitsy was charged with the deaths by neglect of her five-month-old twins.

Brenda had given me the lowdown on her before the first time I visited Bitsy in her cell, at the end of felony block.

"The little twit starved those babies to death! No father, natch, probably screwing around with who knows how many guys. She had Welfare, food stamps, no reason in the world to let those babies die, except she was just too damned lazy and selfish. Women like that oughta be sterilized before they hit puberty!"

Twit or not, she clearly wasn't a danger to anybody on these premises, so she was allowed to come back to my office.

"Hey, this is real pretty."

"They let me fix it up. The County paid for the carpet and cushions, and I found that Monet—the big picture there."

I gestured toward the back of the room, where, nearly covering the entire wall, was a six-by-five-foot reproduction of a woman and a little girl, in hats and long, white dresses, strolling through a meadow of tall grass and red poppies, behind them soft blue sky with a few whiffs of cloud.

"That's real pretty. That's the first pretty thing I've seen since I been here. They wouldn't pay for no chairs?"

"I just liked the idea of cushions better. Have a seat, why don't you?"

Bitsy folded her small, shapely body down onto one of the big cushions. I took one across from her, about two feet of space between us.

Bitsy sat in lotus position, without apparent strain. Unlike most people at their first counseling session, she appeared relaxed, totally comfortable.

There was a moment of pure, lovely silence. (That was the best thing about that sad little excuse for an office: just outside was the bullpen, where the deputies worked at their type-writers and computers, phones rang, misdemeanor inmates came to the counter to make loud demands, or lined up to make their one phone call per day at a wall-mounted pay phone. Vacuum cleaners and waxing machines whirred, trying to bring some sheen to the old vinyl tile floor; cell doors clanged shut. The deputies and prisoners alike were lambasted by the racket all day long. But inside my little sanctum, it was silent as an empty church.)

I never began with talking about an alleged crime; inmates were usually much more obsessed with the more immediate problems of being in jail: anxious about going to court, depen-dent on a harassed, overloaded public defender, their kids going to foster homes or to relatives. They'd often lost all their stuff to their dope-fiend friends who'd come in and cleaned out their apartments as soon as the word got round they'd been busted.

I might or might not get into the crime with them later, and most of the time, as in all prisons everywhere, each woman was convinced she hadn't done the thing she'd got busted for. Lots of other ones, maybe, she'd admit, but not that particular one. They were convinced it wasn't fair.

"Well, how you doin' in here, Bitsy?"

"It's real nice. For a jail, I mean." She smiled; she had pretty, small white teeth. "Everybody treats me real good. I sure do like the food, 'specially that macaroni-cheese like we had today."

"You have any idea when your trial's coming up?"

"No, but my lawyer says it's gonna take a long time. He says it's better to give people some time to kinda forget what happened. We do it right away, people more apt to blame me."

"It must be so hard to lose two little babies."

Bitsy turned off her smile almost mechanically, aware she was not supposed to be enjoying herself when the subject of her children came up. But clearly, joy was a much more natural emotion to her than gloom.

"Ms. Harwood—can I call you Jan? I heard everybody call you that."

"Yes, Jan's fine."

"Jan, I miss those babies terrible. Shawna and little Kaisha. They was the sweetest, prettiest little babies in the world."

We were both silent. Bitsy looked around the tiny, bright room, her eyes lighting on the Monet, where she seemed to fix on the white, floating figures of mother and daughter.

"You want to talk about what happened to them?" I asked softly.

"Nothin' to tell, I guess. They just got sick and died. They'd been cryin' a lot, and didn't want their bottles, and I took 'em to the hospital, but they said it was too late. They couldn't do nothin' for 'em. Kaisha died first, she was the littlest."

"Were you trying to take care of newborn twins all by yourself, Bitsy?"

"No," she smiled, incandescent. "I got a husband. Walter. Well, anyway, he live with me. My mama, she's up Sacramento, she'da helped me, but she got four little ones of her own, and a couple half-grown. I wish she'da been here . . ." her voice trailed off, and for a moment I felt her genuine sadness—her lostness.

"You miss your mama."

"Well, she got a husband, too, and he don't like her comin' down here, and I never had the money to go to Sacramento and see her . . ."

Bitsy suddenly unfolded herself and rose lightly to her feet.

"Well, I'll go back to my cell now. It was nice talkin' to you," she grinned.

I craned my neck up at her, puzzled at her breaking off the session so suddenly. "You've still got a few minutes. We could talk a little more."

"That's okay. I'll go back now."

I pulled myself upright, not so smooth as Bitsy. "If you want to talk some more tomorrow, I'm here."

"That's okay. Nothin' to talk about, really. People are so *nice* in here."

"Well, I'm glad you feel that way. Lots of the women don't."

"I'm just happy to be a place where nobody fusses at me. One of them women in the cell across the hall there called me 'baby-killer' when they first brought me in, but now she's my friend, gave me some pretty pink yarn. I don't know how to crochet yet, but she's gonna teach me when we go to exercise."

I walked back with Bitsy, noticing that several women called out to her in a friendly way from their cells as we passed. Women who are accused of hurting their children don't usually get that kind of treatment; they're cursed at, spat on, hated by all the "good mothers" in the place; but Bitsy had a way about her, and it seemed as though everybody's good mother was evoked by it.

———

Before I left that evening, Darlene, a stocky little deputy who combined a gentle manner with efficient dispatch of her duties, hurried up to me.

"Jan, the lieutenant's called a special meeting for first thing in the morning. 8 A.M. in the Deputy Lounge." She lowered her voice. "She's gonna climb all over you about that incident today."

"Incident? You mean the thing with Tina?"

"Yeah. She's really ticked. Wants you to meet with all of us. I'm sure glad I'm not in your shoes, honey. That's one scary woman."

"What's she ticked about? I prevented a violent incident..."

"That's the way *you* see it, honey, but the lieutenant—and *most* of us, to tell the truth—think you stuck your big nose in where it didn't have no business to be. You could've caused yourself—or a lot of other people—to get hurt bad."

I was flabbergasted. Apparently, I would be officially reprimanded—maybe even *fired* from the jail job—over a thing like this?

The idea stupefied me, but I was convinced that I had done the appropriate thing, using skills that much experience with out-of-control clients had led me to do without thinking twice. It was obvious to me that upset people needed to be handled with care, and calmness—not threats and physical violence! But, of course, I supposed, a cop's training was pretty much the opposite.

Oh, well, I reminded myself, this wasn't really my dream job, anyway—I could simply return to a quiet clinic, where everyone generally maintained a professional, or deferential, demeanor, depending on their degrees and the documents on their walls.

I arrived at work the next morning promptly at eight, prepared, as I thought, by my own convictions, as well as by a friendly pep-talk on the phone from a former supervisor, an older woman I liked and trusted. Though she'd never worked in a jail, she'd been wrangling with the System much longer than I had, she'd taken firm stands in controversies with some tough administrators. She was sympathetic—and slightly amused at the absurdity of my situation, encouraged me to be humble, to show due respect for the expertise of the jail staff in dealing with dangerous situations—but, as I had already decided—not to back down from my view of the incident.

The deputy's "lounge" was actually their restroom—long and narrow, with a row of grey-metal doors to the toilets along one wall, three sinks on the opposite wall, and a small cupboard with an urn and instant coffee makings and styrofoam cups on its top.

Two metal tables were pushed together in the center of the space, with metal folding chairs placed around them. I walked in, pleased at being on time, to find that all ten day-shift deputies and Lieutenant Bramley were already well into the meeting, coffee cups half-drunk, a couple of sheets of paper in front of each of them.

"Well, Jan, you finally made it," the lieutenant said with plenty of attitude.

I glanced at my watch and started to protest that I was on time but decided to keep quiet. My own idea of time and other people's, I'd often noticed, tended to vary—theirs usually less elastic.

"I'll just get some coffee." I went over to the cupboard and made myself some of the harsh, inky brew. I'd been tolerated by the deputies up to now—which was the most I'd hoped for, till they got to know and trust me—but this morning, I felt their open hostility; their collective eyes seemed to be drilling the back of my red cardigan.

They'd saved me a seat near the bottom end of the joined tables, between Marta and Brenda. Neither of the two deputies turned toward me as I slipped into the chair, but Brenda put a sheet of paper in front of me. It was headed, "Breach of Security in Crisis Management of a Felony Prisoner, 9/18/83."

Lieutenant Bramley sat at the other end of the table, intimidating as always in her fitted navy-blue uniform with its touches of polished brass. Her fair red-haired complexion was flushed and her eyes hard.

"All right, let's get on with this business. We've got a ton of other items to cover this morning, deputies. We really can't afford to waste time with *this*, but since yesterday, when you, Jan, decided to step in, take your own life and that of many others into your hands, I have no choice but to take time out of a crowded schedule to let you know that you are in grave jeopardy in your assignment at this facility."

I noticed how shallow my breath was; I inhaled deeply, to relax my tight stomach muscles and allowed some of the tension to slide away with my exhale. My voice came out sounding fairly steady.

"I'm sorry, Lieutenant Bramley, I don't understand what the problem is. I defused a tense situation and got an upset inmate back into her cell without a violent episode."

The lieutenant slipped her gold-rimmed glasses on and referred with a nod to a copy of the "Breach of Security."

"My deputies state that, on the contrary, Jan, you *intervened* in a *potentially dangerous* situation that was *already under control*; they were there in a *damage-control posture* and were about to effect the safe conduct of the inmate into her cell. When you stepped in, you put the whole situation into jeopardy, as the inmate might have injured you or put you under restraint as a *hostage*, thus leading to far more *disastrous consequences!*" Her lips were tight, her voice shaking with anger.

"As I said, Lieutenant, I regret that I didn't know the appropriate protocol—but, you see, I *do know Tina*," I said, keeping my voice mild. "She's not really a violent person, and she trusts me. I was certain she'd follow my advice and my lead. She was very, very frightened; the deputies who were running at her with nightsticks panicked her."

Before I'd quite finished, several deputies began protesting my words, and through the confusion, Brenda's indignant basso voice prevailed.

"The inmate was out of control, Lieutenant, no way she was gonna get back in that cell without three or four of us shovin' her in there!"

Brenda turned and glared at me through narrow dark eyes.

"But she *did*," I said quietly.

"You were very, very *lucky*," Lieutenant Bramley said. "This incident went your way, but it could have gone exactly the opposite! You have to understand that we have prescribed, proven procedures for handling these savages, who sometimes, as a matter of course, go out of control.

"If anything like this ever happens again, Ms. Harwood, you can be *sure* that it will be your *last day in this facility!*

"Now, deputies," she moved right along, choosing a new sheet of paper from the stack in front of her, "we come to the matter of vacation leaves, which are looming ahead of us. Jan," she tossed at me, "you're welcome to stay if you wish, but the rest of the meeting is strictly staff business."

I was still sitting there, mouth open, ready to defend non-violent crisis intervention to the death! But the meeting had moved on, and so must I.

At least, I hadn't been canned—yet. In any case, it was obvious that yesterday's patent demonstration of the superiority of my method had made no impact whatever on the jail's system.

I slid my chair back with a loud scraping noise, nearly knocking my untouched cup of coffee into Brenda's blue-clad lap, but I caught it just in time. As I stood, I felt a light pat on the back of my shoulder and glanced around to see Marta give me a quick, dead-pan wink.

Going To Jail—Part 2

"Bye, darlin', don't forget, seven sharp tomorrow!" I opened the car door. Sam leaned toward me and gave me a deep, sweet kiss.

"Play it cool, babe. Remember, you did the crime, you can do the time."

"Yeah, yeah."

He watched as I walked with scarcely a qualm toward the unwelcoming entrance of the ugly jail building, then waited till I had been admitted before he drove away.

I was thinking how how much worse this would be for somebody entering as an inmate for the first time; I actually felt rather lucky to be armed with knowledge of the layout, the monotony and drabness of the Misdemeanor area where I'd be held, the fattening food, the prickly lieutenant in charge. I wasn't worried in the least by the guards, who, during my two-year tenure as jail counselor, had become much more likely to handle inmates with persuasion rather than threats of mayhem —though neither they nor Lieutenant had mentioned this rather remarkable shift to me.

In fact, as soon as the guard at the door spotted me through the heavy glass peephole, she gave me a big grin and said, "Well, come on in, Jan! *Long time no see!* How ya *been*, girl?"

She buzzed me through, and I recognized her as Marta, one of the hard-core deputies who used to cut me no slack.

"Hi, Marta! You look great, you must have had a good vacation this summer. How are the kids?"

"Yeah, they're cool—we went to Maui! Get this tan!" She held her muscular arms out to me to admire in her short-sleeved summer uniform.

I was astonished by the warmth of her welcome: does she think *I'm coming back for a visit to the old plantation?*

"Ah, Marta, I guess nobody told you—I'm here this time to pay my dues to society—I'm an inmate."

"Well, of course you are! We been waitin' for you since you got sentenced. It's good to have you back!"

"Huh! Well, thanks—I guess. I'm not sure I can say it's real good to *be* back."

Marta guffawed and put her arm through mine. "Let's go get you signed in."

At the office bullpen, several deputies came over to me with smiles and welcome-backs. While we chatted, I signed myself in and turned my purse over to be kept safe (from me and the rest of the boarders) for the next twenty-four hours. I looked around for the faces of familiar inmates, but they were all at breakfast in the dining room.

Marta had gone back to door duty, but Kathy, a young deputy I hadn't worked with, lightly patted me down, escorted me to the shower room and waited while I undressed, used the harsh jail shampoo in the shower, and dressed in jail garb. Then she showed me my bunk in the Misdemeanor dorm, an upper, near the far end of one of the two long rows.

"Okay? If you need an extra pillow or anything, let me know."

She added, rather shyly. "You're pretty famous around here."

I laughed. "No kidding? I wonder what for? Thanks, Kathy, I was dreading the shower and the processing stuff, but it wasn't bad at all. Can I get my book and my notebook and pen back? They're in my purse."

"Sure, just go ask 'em."

The door to the dorm was never closed, except at night and in cases of emergency; most of the time, its occupants were free to walk out into the central area to speak to the guards there.

I returned to the bullpen, and as I started back to my bunk

with my innocuous belongings, a slender whirlwind of wiry red hair and crisp uniform swooped at me, threw an arm over my shoulders and exclaimed, "*Jan Harwood!* When I saw your name on the booking sheet, I knew it had to be for some noble cause!"

It was Lieutenant Bramley, will wonders never cease? I needed a few moments to find my tongue; then I laughed and warmly greeted this stern little woman who had never, before now, let drop the slightest hint that she admired me or my work.

———

At exactly seven the next morning, Sam collected me, happy that I was back intact. He wanted to hear all about my day in the slammer. But I wasn't ready to talk about it for a few days, except in the most general terms.

It took a while for me to process the catharsis I had unexpectedly experienced: taking the shower, eating the food, sleeping in the bunk, wearing the clothes, and most significantly, being well and truly locked in—seemed to have resolved some existential burden I'd been carrying around since my first day working in the jail.

It was only twenty-four hours, but somehow, I had, at last, been released.

Patchouli, 1976

Here I am, scribbling again. I'm not even sure why I've kept this diary for nearly thirty years. I don't write in it every day—more like two-three times a week. I sure don't want anyone else to read it! Heavens, *no*—it'd kill me if anybody else ever got hold of it! I didn't even start it till the kids grew up and moved out, because I knew that wherever I stashed it, one of them would turn it up—like they say about guns in the house.

I've never had to worry about Del that way, he's not one to poke around, just wants things the same every day—his clean clothes, the paper, his scotch, his dinner and the remote; he's happy as long as everything is exactly where he found it the day before. I keep my diary under my side of the mattress—he'd die before he'd make a bed, so it's safe. The old books that I've already filled up are in a shoe box—it's the boot box my long green-suede boots came in—it's a lot bigger and sturdier than your average shoe-box—in the crawlspace under the roof. I know whenever he's going to go up there to check out a leak or the wiring or something, and I get it down and hide it under the plastic bags in the basement that I keep my "someday" quilt scraps in.

I know I ought to burn those books. I'm still healthy as a horse, but you just never know what kind of nasty little twisted cell might be sitting in your ovaries or your colon—and then there's strokes and heart attacks—plenty of my friends have already succumbed to one thing or another. Del and I've already made our wills, and we both filled out those medical forms for if you don't want to be kept alive after you're dead in every way that counts. I sure don't, and I've told my kids and my doctor, so I hope there won't be any argument about it.

But I haven't quite made up my mind to burn my diaries yet. Sometimes I like to look back at my life during a special time—like when Jeannie got married, and when Lilly, our first grandbaby, was born—to see how I felt then. It helps me when I'm sad—which isn't often, but it does creep up on a person sometimes, after a certain age.

To tell the truth, there's nothing much in them that wouldn't bore anybody to death—mostly normal, daily stuff. Jeannie might glance through 'em, and throw 'em in the trash; the boys probably wouldn't even be that interested.

Unless, heaven forbid, one of them happened onto that time in—must've been '72 or '73—when I took that crazy class at the Community Center, that the lady from County Mental Health, Jan, her name was—ran for women like me. I'm still amazed that I ever got myself to sign up for it!

My doctor told me about it one time when I was crying on her shoulder about how Del was being so mean— threatening to leave me just on account of sex! I couldn't see what he had to complain about. I was willing, most any time he wanted it, same as always. Sex was no big whoop for me—never had been —but unless I was worn to a complete frazzle—like I probably was pretty often when I was chauffeuring the kids around to all their games and things, and working part-time in the school cafeteria—that really took it out of me—I always let him do whatever he wanted. I liked that he got so excited doing it, and it was nice being close to him.

But then, over the years, he kind of lost interest, and since I couldn't care less, we just about stopped.

But that was just at the times when S-E-X was all you ever heard about! The Hippies, "free love," wife-swapping, orgies, love-ins and all—plus TV and movies were all about Sex, Sex, Sex! Del got it into his head that he was missing out. We'd never really even talked about our sex life before—but all of a sudden, he wanted me to do things I'd never even heard of, much less tried! He brought home this book, *The Joy of Sex*—it was all I could do to look at the pictures. I couldn't believe how worked up he got.

"All you ever do is just lay there," he yelled at me. Well, that's all he ever wanted before, and I thought that's all there was to it—I really did—at least for *decent* people! I knew there were prostitutes who did nasty things, but I couldn't believe he wanted his own wife to act like that! I told him I was sorry, if he couldn't be satisfied with me, he could just go to one of those women downtown, but he said, no, he didn't want to do that, but he wasn't so old that he couldn't find himself a different wife!

"I love you, Marilee," he told me, "but there's plenty of husbands these days that are having a lot of fun. There's nice girls and women, some of 'em work right with me in the office every day, that'd be happy to sleep with a guy like me; I hear 'em talking all the time. They're on the Pill and they can do it with anybody they want to. I was never unfaithful to you yet, and wouldn't want to be. But if something doesn't change—

well, you know how many of our friends have split up in the past few years."

I sure did. Many of the couples we knew, the men had turned in their wives for a newer model. I just never thought it could happen to Del and me. We've been together so long, I believed we were flesh of each other's flesh—I think that's in the Bible—not just connected by a piece of paper. I cried and yelled, and I asked him, just exactly *what* was it he expected me to *do*?

"I can't be younger than I am!" I told him! "I'm forty-six, just like you, and I've got grey hair, and these sags and bags. If you want some young starlet —"

"No, Marilee, all I want is you. But I want both of us to have a good time in bed—I want you to *enjoy* it. You know, hon," he says, "I've never even heard you yell out when you *come*!"

Even writing those words was almost impossible; I guess I thought the paper might burst into flame.

But there was nobody I could *tell* about it, so I put it all down, all my tears and anger, and the terrible fear that he meant what he said about leaving.

But then, writing it down made me think about our "sex life" and I realized that I wasn't sure that I'd *ever* actually "*come*."

I knew what he meant of course, because *he* surely got there, every time! He'd start out slow, then he'd get to pumping harder and faster, panting and grunting—working himself up to a big finish. It always seemed like he'd lost his mind there for a few minutes; it was kind of scary. Me, I was just waiting him out, and happy to be done with it.

But I'd been hearing on Phil Donahue that the *woman* is supposed to get a big thrill, too—he called it an "orgasm"—but I just thought that was women's lib talk, since now, all of a sudden, women were supposed to be equal to men.   I wondered, how could a woman build up a head of steam, squashed flat under a hundred and eighty pounds of man? I didn't have a clue. I guessed that I just wasn't born with *it*, whatever *it* was.

But then I went to my doctor for a Pap smear, and when she asked me when did I last have intercourse, I busted out in tears, told her I wasn't made right or something, and my husband was going to leave me, and she patted my shoulder and told me about this class run by the County, for *"Pre-orgasmic Women."* I could hardly believe the government was putting on that kind of program, but sure enough, when I checked, they said it was starting up the next Tuesday at the Community Center downtown. So, just to show Del I was trying, I signed up.

It turned out there were nine others in the class, all kinds of women, but I was probably the oldest. Most looked as scared and shame-faced as I was, that first meeting—nobody could look anybody else in the eye.

But the teacher, her name was Jan, said it was natural to feel that way at first. She got us to telling about ourselves, our kids and husbands and jobs, and why we signed up for the course, and after a while I got more relaxed. I was surprised to hear all the other ladies come right out and say *they'd* never had an "orgasm," either. Some said they wanted to have those wild, fantastic feelings they'd heard about, and others, like me, just wanted to get better at sex to please their men. I'd *never* heard women speak out like that in public before—even on Donahue! I've got to say, it was a great comfort to know I wasn't the only one!

Jan said we'd meet for ten weeks, and by that time—if we faithfully did our *one hour of homework a day,* she was sure we'd learn how to *"orgasm."* (I pictured this big stack of books we'd have to read, but I was determined to go through with the class, just to show Del, even though I didn't expect to get much out of it.) Laura mentioned that it might take a little extra time to "transfer the experience to sex with our partners." That puzzled me, until she showed us the movie.

This real pleasant-looking woman, wearing only a plain bathrobe, talked straight to us about she'd never been real comfortable with her body, hadn't liked it very much because it wasn't just perfect, and how, in a class like ours, she'd learned to appreciate it. Then she goes on—it's still kind of embarrassing to admit it, because I was taught it's wicked to think much of yourself—not to mention to *love* your own body! Well, then, this woman just takes her robe off—she's stark naked!—and begins to touch herself—her face, breasts, shoulders, arms and legs, her belly—even her feet—stroking them softly, like a lover! Then she lays down on the bed and spreads her legs apart in a way that no *lady would ever do, and starts to caress herself there, very, very gently*.

Then the camera zooms in, and you see—goodness, just *thinking* about it gets me all hot and bothered!—you see her *thing*, her *pussy's* what Del calls it (my mom just called it "down there," or "possible," as when taking a bath, you wash down as far as possible and up as far as possible, and then you wash 'possible"). But Jan called it a "vagina," which I still don't think is a very nice word, but it *is* the scientific word, so I say it now, even to my little granddaughter, once, when the subject came up at the ladies' room at the movies.

Anyway, this lady in the video's vagina, up close, looked so complicated, not exactly pretty, but sort of exotic, like one of those purple orchids with two big petals cupping a set of rosy-pink ones; then the camera moved in even closer, and we saw something *I* didn't even know was *down* there—a little bright pink thing, like the very end of your tongue! She began stroking it with her finger, and you could see it actually getting bigger, just like a tiny penis; she rubbed in little circles around it at first, then harder and harder, you could her moaning louder and louder as it swelled up—and finally, the camera rolled back; you saw her whole body grow stiff, and she got this look on her face like she was in bliss and agony, both at the same time, and she groaned, really loud at first, then faded to a quiet moan. Then she threw her head and arms back and relaxed on the bed, smiling at the camera in a very satisfied way.

I could not believe I was sitting there with strangers, all probably just as shocked as I was, watching that shameless woman, stark naked, *masturbating* herself! But Jan said we could call it "pleasuring," that there's nothing wrong with it, it's your body, after all and it's made to give you pleasure. Especially, that little pink thing, she called it a "clitoris." I was pretty sure I didn't have one—that must be what's missing, I thought. I wondered if this class was going to be watching dirty movies and supposedly, getting turned on by them. If so, it sure wouldn't work for me!

Jan asked us what we thought about the movie. Nobody could even talk at first, but this redheaded girl of about thirty, said, "I thought it was real *embarrassing*—but it must be just wonderful to feel like that!"

Then everybody wanted to talk at once, saying they could never do that, or how they'd tried it once but didn't get anywhere with it. I was too mortified to say a word.

Finally, our teacher gave us our "homework" assignment for the week: every single day, including weekends, we had to take one hour just for ourselves—lock ourself in the bathroom, if necessary, and take a nice, long bath, with bubbles or bath salts or oil. We couldn't even use a washrag, but just our hands to soap ourselves up. We were supposed to stroke our whole bodies, *lovingly,* that was the teacher's word—like the lady did in the film. Everybody protested, how did she suppose that mothers with little kids, or nosy husbands, and a million things to do—how were we supposed to find a *whole hour* out of a day?

"Now, that," Jan said, "right there is a big part of the problem—a lot of us women never get the time to relax and enjoy ourselves, but with all we *do,* it's something we *need* and *deserve!*" I had to agree with her there. Of course, I had more time than a lot of them, now that the kids were grown, but there was always plenty to do. It wouldn't have occurred to me in a million years to take a long bath in the middle of the day!

She went on, "Now, this is important: when you get out of the tub, dry off and go stand naked in front of a full-length mirror—or the longest one you've got—and just look at yourself —not the way you usually do, criticizing your stretch marks or your droopy breasts. Just look at yourself as if you were from Mars, and never saw a human body before. Just *marvel at* the wonderful way it's made, and all the things it can do! And, if there's a part of your body you especially don't like, smooth it with baby oil or lotion, and *talk nice to it*"—or something crazy like that. I could just see me, talking baby talk to my varicose veins, or my big butt!

But at least, she didn't tell us to do anything real disgusting, so I decided I'd try the baths. She said we could read, listen to the radio, or whatever—and I had a whole stack of *McCall's* Magazine to catch up on.

So I went along with it for that whole week, and it was very nice and relaxing, but I couldn't see how it was going to save my marriage. But it was interesting to see how the other ladies were doing, so I went back the next week.

Everybody reported on their fancy baths, and how surprised they were that they'd managed to find an hour, or most of one, every day. They were excited and looking forward to next week's "homework." I was still expecting Jan to pass out a bunch of books, but she said the homework was to start "exploring ourselves," which turned out to mean feeling around "down there," to find all the parts we saw the woman touching in the movie—including that "clitoris" thing. She said that little bitty thing was the key to a woman's "climax," and that, right after our bath, we should scoot right up to a mirror—can you imagine?—and spend some time *getting familiar* with "that very special part of our beautiful bodies."

Then everybody started talking about how they were taught to be ashamed of their private parts, and it was pretty upsetting to hear the awful things that had been said and done to some of those girls. All I remember is mama telling me that a nice girl should never touch "down there," except with toilet paper when she had to.

I never spoke up in class. I didn't see how I could ever poke around down there—but Del kept asking me, how was I doing? Was the class any good, when did I think I'd be ready to try it out on him? So I kept doing the "homework," and, by golly, I found out that I *do* have one of those clitoris things, which is real sensitive, although I never did get it to swell up like in the movie. After awhile, I could hardly wait for the next class, because by the end of the third week, some of the girls said they were feeling new things; one woman even said she'd actually *had* one, rubbing like the movie woman—and it was fantastic! And every week after that, more of the students reported that they'd *got there!*

But rub as hard or as soft as I might, not much happened for me. Jan mentioned things we could try—like—Lord, this is embarrassing!—tickling yourself with a soft feather, or using K-Y jelly for lubrication, or imagining yourself with a real sexy guy. (I tried to imagine Del at first, but that didn't work at all—so then I tried Paul Newman, and I'm ashamed to admit it, but I did get a little rise out of him!)

By the eighth week, the only other ones who hadn't had an orgasm were me and this other woman, Sheila, who was actually the sexiest-looking girl in the class. She had long, dyed red hair, wore the tiniest miniskirts, low-cut blouses and spike heels —but Jan told her that she was afraid Sheila was never going to get there unless she cut her fingernails. They were nearly two inches long, so long they curled under at the ends. But she wouldn't do it, she said they weren't a problem, she could type and wash dishes or whatever, and her boyfriend thought they were beautiful. Jan sighed, and told her she'd just have to work around 'em.

"So what about you, Marilee?" Jan asked. "You haven't said anything. Are you doing your homework faithfully?" I said I was, but it wasn't doing any good.

"Have you tried all the suggestions I've given, like bubble-baths with scented candles, some nice music? Have you let yourself fantasize a very romantic lover?"

"Yes, ma'am, I did most of that. Except, I never tried the candles."

She gave me this warm, compassionate look, and said gently, "Well, Marilee, you just keep on practicing everything you've learned, every day, and I'm sure that any day now, you're going to have the most wonderful orgasms!"

But I could tell she didn't really think so. I'm sure she could see just from the way I dressed—my navy-blue slacks and cardigan, the black Oxford shoes, my mostly grey hair permed like my mom and her friends wore at my age—that I just wasn't a sexy-type person. But by now, I *really wanted* to make it—not just for Del—or even for myself—but also for teacher Jan, because I knew she really wanted a 100% success rate for her class.

I stopped at a hippy shop on my way home and bought a

candle scented with patchouli, which I thought was more exotic than rose or lilac—and I went right home and tried it out.

I wanted to see what I wrote in my diary that day, so this morning I climbed up and got down my boot box.

The pages for 1973 are getting a little yellow around the edges, but you can still read them, even though *that* day, for some reason, I wrote with a mechanical pencil we had lying around—do they even make those anymore? Well, anyway, here's what it says:

"Oh, my good Lord, thank you, thank you, thank you! Thank you for the County Mental Health and thank you for the rest of the ladies in the class, and especially thank you for my teacher! I never dreamed anything could make me feel so wild and free and young —and *beautiful*—and very, very happy! If I'd had any idea what I was missing! It's just tragic, that's all, to go so many years without knowing how it feels to get all worked up so bad, every second more exciting than the one before. You're climbing higher and higher and you feel like, just one more move and you're going to reach a place more glorious, more fantastic than you could ever imagine: it's right there! It's going to happen, *now*—and then it doesn't, but it *almost does*, so you keep on and keep on, and it builds back up again to that place where something—you can't imagine exactly *what*—and still it doesn't— but there's no way in the world you're gonna stop now—so you push, push it in harder and faster, faster—you wiggle around it and every place it touches feels sweeter than Mrs. See's best chocolates—you want to hold and squeeze your own breasts because every inch of you is so turned on, you wish you could kiss your breasts, your nipples are sticking out like they did when they were bursting with milk for your babies—and then, suddenly—it's like—like a rocket bursting with colors, all the joy you ever had in your lifetime happening at once—you have to scream and laugh and cry at the same time!

"And then it's over, but not completely, not for a long time; you still feel—creamy, kind of, like there was a glow coming from you and everything around you.

"I can't wait to tell Jan and the girls! I really should tell Del first, I guess, but I don't think I want to let him in on it on it, just yet. I want to keep it all to myself for a little while—see if I can make it happen again! Also, I'm not sure how he'll feel about the candle. But I guess he'll be happy to learn there's nothing wrong with me. THERE'S NOT A SINGLE THING WRONG WITH ME, that's for darn sure! Now I understand that song, '*I am woman—hear me roar!*' *Thank you, Lord!*"

Whew! I sure hope nobody ever gets hold of that one. Jeanie'd have a heart attack—although I sometimes think it'd do her good to read something like that. Maybe I won't burn them —not right away, anyhow.

I told Del the next day, at breakfast—I couldn't keep a big secret from my oldest and dearest friend—and he got so excited that he called in sick to work, and we went right back to bed together, something that *never* happened even when we were newlyweds. We started out using the candle, but after he figured out how that worked, we tried it without, and that went just fine, too. We spent the whole day in bed—called out for Chinese at dinnertime, and for a few days after that, we ate nothing but delivery. We were crazy in love all over again!

That's when I bought those thigh-high green suede boots, and I lightened up my hair a little so it was more blond than grey, and I got me some pretty new dresses, short, like they wore 'em then. Naturally, things calmed down some after a while; but our lovemaking has just got better over the years— more tender, deeper, more understanding.

And once in a great while, when Del's away fishing or

something, I get to thinking about Paul Newman, when he was young—or that handsome fella that was on "ER"—George Clooney?—and I get in a little practice, just on my own.

I never did hear if Sheila got there. She didn't come to the last class. If she had of, I would've told her she didn't need to cut her nails, all she needed was a candle. I'd recommend patchouli.

Gambling with Mom, 1996

I was awakened by the cat's stirring in the curve of my knees, and the sound of my mother's slippered footfalls, stopping at my partly open bedroom door.

She's just standing there, watching me. I shuddered.

The slippers didn't move away, and after a few moments, I opened my eyes to a blur of morning sunlight..

"What is it, Mom?" I shouted hoarsely.

Now that I was retired and not slave to an alarm clock, I liked to wake up slowly, uttering my first words softly to T.S. Elliott, the black-and-grey tabby.

Mom's voice, cracked by age and over-loud because of her hearing loss, was artificially cheery.

"You better get up and get ready, if we're going to catch the plane. I'd make coffee, but I don't understand your fancy French coffeepot."

"Just heat the water and pour it over the grounds, Mom—and our flight isn't till one this afternoon."

I slid my legs out from under the covers and pulled myself up to sit on the edge of the bed. Elliott, unfazed by this break in the morning ritual, leapt down and headed for the kitchen to check his bowl.

"You better do it, honey, I'd just make a mess."

My mother, Lucy, had become greatly enfeebled over the past year. I'd been shocked by the changes in her when I picked her up at the San Francisco Airport a few days before. Her shoulders were hunched and her back bent. Her skin was very pale, almost grey, until she put on her foundation and rouge each morning. Even the excitement of her annual visit had restored little of her usual vitality.

I put on my bathrobe and followed her to the kitchen. She had already dressed and made up her face for our trip to a new gambling casino in Central California. Mom had read about it in her Miami newspaper; it was owned and operated by Native Americans of some unspecified tribe and was said to be making them rich. One thing Mom always wanted to do when she came out was to go gambling, and in years before, we had taken an excursion bus or driven to Tahoe or Reno. Mom would spend two or three days—and well into the nights—playing the nickel slots, usually coming away with a few dollars more than she'd started out with, while I roamed around playing the poker and blackjack machines, or putting clunky official slugs into the dollar slots until I was a couple of hundred in the hole. But it was something she enjoyed, and a way to fill a substantial chunk of those difficult two weeks. We could play at machines an acre apart in those vast, clamorous caverns, where there was no difference between day and night, and we needed to come together and make conversation only at mealtimes and when we agreed it was time to cash in and go to bed.

"That's a pretty outfit," I said loudly, blinking at her peach polyester pantsuit. "I don't think I've seen it before." I turned on the teakettle and measured four spoonsful of coffee into the glass pot.

"Yes, it's brand new! I ordered it from the Blair catalog, but I made the blouse myself—I wasn't sure the salmon in the blouse would match, but, look, it's just perfect! I was so anxious that it wouldn't come in time—but it came just the day before I left home—and I stayed up till midnight hemming the pants. I always have to shorten them."

She patted her small belly, always held in tightly by a strong elastic girdle. She was five-foot-one and came up to my chin.

"Yeah, I know—I do, too."

I also inherited the family big bottom, and now my stomach is starting to look like hers, "without the girdle," I ruefully added to myself. At sixty-five, just two decades younger than my mother, it appalled me to think that in just twenty years, I'd probably look much the way she did now. Her lightly pock-marked face was deeply lined, her neck a mass of crepy folds. Her hair, which she had always dyed with henna, had been wiry and stiff, but now she'd let it turn naturally to an attractive silver, cut short and wavy around her head. An area at the back looked thin, showing her pale scalp.

Mom's light-brown eyes were almost lashless, nearly lost in the droop of her fleshy eyelids. I'd always been vain about my long-lashed dark-brown eyes and hair. L'Oreal, I comforted myself, will deal with the hair, and mascara should salvage my lashes indefinitely! And I'll still have my teeth—I hope!

Lucy had always valued a woman's looks, including mine, above any other virtue. I thought it was because she was so inse-cure about her own appearance, which had been marred by severe acne in her teens, and which tormented her to some degree for another thirty years, until menopause.

We ate cold cereal with sliced bananas and skimmed milk, while Mom described in detail how she had come by all three of the new ensembles she'd bought for her trip, all of them much like the one she had on, except for the colors.

"Ted and Winnie gave me a pretty lavender sweatsuit. Of course, it's always too hot to wear it at home, but it's perfect for here—it's always so cold here."

"So, how are they doing since they got back together?" I asked, more than ready for a change of topic.

"Oh, I guess they're fine. Of course, I don't see them much nowadays." Her voice, pitched much lower now, surprised me by its bitterness.

"You don't? How come?"

My brother and sister-in-law had always treated Lucy as the undisputed matriarch of the family, even before Ted's and my father died some years before. She was very close to the couple's three children (she barely knew mine, which was the way I wanted it) and had always had free run of their home in Central Florida, near the condo that they had bought for her. They'd even set up a small studio in their former laundry room, where she made neatly crafted stained-glass lamps and ornaments.

"I have no idea! They used to have me over for Sunday dinner almost every week, but now I hardly ever get invited—and when I hint, they act like they don't know what I'm talking about!"

"Have you asked them about it, in so many words?"

"Oh, Janny, no! I could never do that! No, if they don't want me, I'll just manage without!"

Her eyes were damp with tears that I knew she wouldn't actually shed, just as her mind was over-stuffed with grievances that she'd never share with those she believed to be the cause of them.

Her voice was low and doleful as she went on, "I don't have much longer, you know. This disease is going to kill me."

She slumped down in her chair, lifted her large-knuckled, capable hands – which had never hesitated to undertake any job, from cooking and sewing to constructing a rock retaining wall, to building B-25s in a bomber plant during the Second World War. Now she scratched vigorously at the thin spot I had noticed, and when she swiveled her neck to reach a targeted area, I saw a streak of raw, dark-red: she'd broken through the tough scalp, and was beginning to ooze blood!

"Mom, please, don't scratch there! You're making a bloody sore back there! And what makes you think an itchy head is going to kill you? Your doctors have told you it's not a serious problem!"

"They don't know anything about it," she exploded furiously. "They admit, they've never seen anything like it before and they don't know how to treat it. They've prescribed all kinds of shampoos and lotions–and I've used them religiously – but none of them does a bit of good! They should have to live with this for just one day, they'd see how serious it is! It started on my head, but now it's spreading all over my body—here, look at my arm!"

She pulled back the sleeve of the bright pink jacket, baring her sun-wrinkled wrist, which was slightly mottled with unpigmented spots. I stared at the arm, almost hoping to see evidence of the plague that my mother had suffered with for nearly two years.

On her visit the year before, I had taken her to see a well-recommended dermatologist. After listening to her complaint, Dr. Whitsell had asked her to sit alone for five minutes in a small, dark room with a blue light. He explained that if, as she believed, there were tiny insects in her scalp, the blue light would bring them to the surface.

Impressed by the doctor's scientific demeanor and self-assurance, she agreed without hesitation.

As soon as the door of the small room closed behind her, the doctor spoke quietly to me about my mother's urgent need to see a psychiatrist.

"You're saying that there's nothing wrong with her scalp?"

"Nope—not a thing! It's a delusion; we sometimes see it in cocaine addicts, who think there are bugs crawling under their skin. I assume your mother doesn't use cocaine?"

I laughed at his solemn expression.

"Mom, using street drugs! Hardly! But she takes a bunch of prescription meds, for blood pressure and heart problems, and her doctors in Florida have prescribed all kinds of foul-smelling stuff to rub on her head!"

"Placebos. They're hoping she'll think the medicines are working and forget about it. But it looks to me as though the delusion is deeply entrenched."

He shook his head and looked professionally doleful.

"She probably just doesn't have enough to do, at her advanced age. But I think some mild antipsychotic medicine, plus an antidepressant, might help."

Fat chance, I thought.

"Well, of course, I'll try, but I can't imagine her agreeing to see a psychiatrist. I've been a psychotherapist for thirty years, but she still thinks therapy is just for crazy people."

I sighed. "It's so strange, you know?—she's as sensible about most things as she ever was."

He let Mom out of her blue closet and made a show of examining her scalp for wildlife. Then he reassured her that, although he didn't know a cure for her condition, he was convinced it would get better in time. She should keep on using her doctors' prescriptions.

(I noticed he didn't say a word to her about psychiatry.)

Lucy had seemed briefly comforted by his words, but the "disease" had not improved over the following year; in fact, during our phone conversations, she had described a dramatic worsening. As I predicted, she wouldn't hear of seeing a psychiatrist. She'd stopped making the beautiful stained-glass objects that had absorbed her since a year or so after my dad died. She'd quit going out to lunch with her few friends or attending potlucks at her condominium complex.   My brother had confided that he and Winnie had reached the limits of their patience with Lucy and her "disease," since that's all she ever talked about these days.

Dr. Whitsell had, it seemed, cured her of the notion of bugs, but now she explained her elaborate new theory.

"See, Janny, there are these patches of hard little lumps, on my head and all over my body—oh, they itch and hurt so bad! Nobody understands the pain I live with! The patches are tied together with long cords that run just under the skin–and I've figured out that if I can just break through the cord, by scratching it really hard—Oh, it hurts so much!–but I have to do it, because if I break a cord, the lumps just go away!"

I knew from experience with clients that it's useless to try to talk a deluded person out of a delusion—but I'd done my best to convince Mom that her fierce scratching only made the problem worse, and, in fact, was probably the sole cause of the pain that sometimes kept her awake all night.

I pushed my chair back from the breakfast table and began to collect our dishes.

"I am sorry that you're suffering, Mama," I said, meaning it sincerely.

"But, now, we're going to have three whole days–and nights, just for fun, food and debauchery! We'll get free cocktails all day long, and try to score some big bucks!"

"Yes, sure, that sounds real nice . . ." she agreed; but her voice was dull, and her hand had found its way back to the tender spot at the back of her head.

———

The casino was brand new, and huge, with Las Vegas-type decor meant to assure people that California farm country was just as glamorous as the Nevada desert for gambling. On the marquee, which could be seen for a very long distance across level fields and orchards, neon lights in garish colors flashed in sequence to create a great fountain, spouting golden coins. The airport bus let us off in front of the building, where immaculate uniformed valets ferried our bags to a room on the third floor.

Inside the casino, I cringed at the sounds and sights of hundreds of new electronic machines, clustered in rows of twenty-five-cent, fifty-cent, dollar and five-dollar categories, stretching as far as the eye could see in the pall of cigarette smoke. The machines flashed with ripples of multicolored light, making eerie, outer-space noises whenever a coin was dropped into a slot, and discs carrying images of fruit or clowns or big sevens began to roll. Whenever somebody won some coins, a cylindrical plastic cap on top of the machine flashed brilliant yellow, and a raucous trill informed the entire establishment that there was another lucky winner. There was an indistinct rumble of voices, too, although everyone I could see was communing only with a machine.

"No one-armed bandits here, Mom," I shouted into her ear. "They're all push-buttons—and I don't see any nickel slots."

"Oh, shoot! I like to pull the arm on the old machines! These aren't near as much fun."

But as soon as we had checked into our room, used the bathroom and tidied our hair, we took the swift elevator back down into the bedlam of the casino. Lucy soon found a quarter machine that kept her breaking even for hours, while I began my customary search for a poker machine that was rigged in the customers' favor.

We met, as agreed, at six o'clock in the lavish, but shockingly inexpensive "buffet"—whatever it took to bring people back to gamble!—where each of us reported having lost an acceptably small amount of money. We were both enthusiastic, but normally healthy eaters, regarding these annual sojourns as occasions to gorge ourselves on the sort of salt-fat-grease-and-sugar-laden fare we avoided the rest of the year.

I tucked into my heaped-up plate with enthusiasm, hoping I could stuff down enough of this gaudy but delicious-smelling feast to justify returning, a bit later, to the madly decadent dessert banquette.

Then I saw that Lucy had laid down her fork after taking only a few bites of her rib roast and mashed potatoes–she hadn't touched the sliced ham, green beans and pickled beets she'd piled on her dish.

"What's wrong, Mom?–you'd better eat up, I saw you ogling that coconut-custard meringue pie back there . . ."

She didn't indicate that she'd heard me: she was digging around in her white leather purse, and in a moment pulled out a long metal nail file with a pointed tip. She reached behind her head and began jabbing furiously at the sore spot, her eyes blank with concentration. She seemed unaware of the dozens of diners who were moving around us with loaded trays, some of whom cast a quick, shocked glance at the crazy-looking old woman, stabbing her own head and groaning in obvious anguish.

I jumped up from my seat and rushed to her, crying, "No! Stop it, Mom, you're really hurting yourself!"—but in her trance-like space she continued to dig until I pulled the file out of her hand, crying myself now, and pleading with her to stop. I pressed a clean napkin against the open sore she'd created, and urged her up and out of the dining room. I was in dread that someone would sound an alarm, drawing medical personnel, maybe even police!

We managed to find a ladies' room, where leather-like benches gave us a chance to rest, and soon, Lucy seemed to regain awareness of the world around her. The bleeding of the small lesion stopped quickly, and to my consternation, Mom announced that she wanted to go back to her favorite electronic bandit and play some more.

"Okay, Mom—but you have to promise me not to touch your poor head any more. You scared me so bad back there!"

"Okay, sure, Janny, I promise. But I don't understand why you get so upset. I'm the one that's suffering."

———

It was nearly one AM when we went back to our room. It was large enough for two double beds, the new furniture and decor was in relatively good taste, and for a casino hotel, the pictures on the walls—subdued scenes of trees and mountains—were not offensive. The carpet, a soft, thick beige, looked immaculate.

I propped two large, over-firm pillows against the head of my bed, and opened a potboiler I'd picked up at the airport. Mom was usually asleep long before I was ready to turn out my bed lamp, but tonight, she was still in the bathroom, applying a smelly lotion to her scalp.

Finally, she approached her bed, wearing a thin, pink night-gown and a shower cap, which, she explained, she had to wear to keep the lotions working during the night. She had removed her false teeth, and her withered face had caved in on itself. She looked closer to a hundred than to eighty-five.

She sat on the edge of her bed, apparently oblivious of me, lying a few feet away, watching her; she inserted her fingers under the elastic at the back of the cap, and began scratching, hard, methodically, with the stubborn determination she had applied to most of the challenges she had encountered in life.

I tried to ignore her, hoping she'd soon crawl under the covers and go to sleep; but I couldn't concentrate on my book, and finally laid it down.

"Mom," I said gently, "Please, don't do that. You promised."

She made no response, and I realized that she hadn't heard me. She'd probably left her hearing aid in the bathroom. I repeated myself, almost shouting, thinking how hard it is to speak compassionately in a loud voice.

"PLEASE, MOM, DON'T SCRATCH! YOU'RE HURTING YOURSELF!"

Startled, she stared at me blankly for a moment, then patted her plastic cap back into place.

"Oh, okay. Goodnight, sleep tight!"

But it took a long while to relax, as I found myself reviewing, for the thousandth time, the complexities of our carefully-constructed relationship. It was easy enough to handle during most of the year, when, on the phone once a week, we exchanged news of Ted's family and mine, talked about the Florida vs. California weather, what she had cooked and eaten that week, or a stained-glass project she was immersed in. She was also a rabid football fan, and proceeded to give me the latest news of the various Florida teams; I spaced out whenever the subject came up.

But her annual two-week visit was another matter. As I had once confided to my friend, Karen, "The hardest thing is that after a few days, I get so angry at her, for no very good reason. She tries to be nice—she's stopped criticizing me or my kids all the time, and she seems to appreciate anything I do for her."

Karen, another therapist, nodded.

"I know. Mothers and daughters—it's so hard."

"It's just that, from the day I was born, she seemed deter-mined to convince me that I was wrong, stupid, clumsy, homely —a mess of a person. And, of course, part of me believed it–she was my Mom. My parents were very young, and life was hard–those were bad Depression times. I felt like she was angry at me, for all the years I lived at home."

"Then you went off to college—"

"Yes, thank God—and from there to New York, and eventu-ally, California. The farther away I got from her, the better I felt—and the better she seemed to tolerate me. . . I had therapy for years, worked hard to deal with these painful issues–and nowadays, I usually consider myself a sound, rational person. But with her, sometimes, I still feel nuts! Why didn't I get past it?"

I let out a small scream, pounded the arm of the sofa.

"It's maddening!"

"Have you ever shared any of this with her, Jan?"

"Oh, heaven forfend! That's part of the original problem— if you ever say one word to my mother about feelings—hers or your own—if you're a kid, you get hit; if you're older, she just ignores you!"

Now, in that immaculate, comfortable, but soulless hotel room, I was acutely aware of my mother's rounded back lying in the bed a few feet from mine. Images of her as a young mother, enraged over some small infraction, smacking my face, chasing me through the house with stinging switches, spanking my bottom until it burned, roughly pulling my hair while trying to untangle it. Though long-banished to the ancient-history vault, these memories still made me clench my fists and bite my lip.

I reminded myself once again that, compared to the vicious child abusers I'd heard about from clients, my mother was simply not in the same realm. In those days, there was no Dr. Spock; the general public possessed very little awareness of child psychology. My mother, originally a farm girl, might have had dreams of a far different life—though she never talked about them—and there she was, stuck in a small house with an overly sensitive child, then another baby— with nothing to do but dull, repetitive housework. My father was tender with her, but his job at the city streetcar company kept him away for eleven hours a day, six days a week.

Lucy's skin was pockmarked to a degree that made her extremely sensitive to others' judgments of her, and wary of anybody who tried to be her friend. When Teddy and I were kids, she spent hours at the bathroom mirror every day working at her pimples with a needle and fingernails, which left her face red and raw as hamburger. We didn't dare approach her with our frequent child needs during those trancelike hours; she was somewhere far away, dreaming of who knows what.

———

I slept for an hour or so but woke up when Mom bumped into something as she shuffled to the bathroom in the near-dark. A bright light came on in there, but the door stayed open, and I rolled away from the mild assault to my eyes, trying to get back to sleep. Dozing, I gradually became aware that she'd been in there for an abnormally long time. The clock on my lamp-table read 3:53.

Outside our room, a group of gamblers walked down the carpeted corridor laughing and talking in loud, drunken-sounding voices, which brought me fully awake.

She's got to stop this!

Without thinking what I was going to do, I got out of bed and strode to the open door, where I saw my mother crouching on the toilet, her back and shoulders deeply hunched and her head hanging down. The shower cap lay beside her feet on the tile floor. Her face was set in an awful grimace of pain, as the strong nails of both hands scraped relentlessly at the back of her head.

In her near-trance state, she didn't see me standing in the doorway. An ancient fury welled up in me, as I clenched my fists and moved a few steps into the room, screaming in rage:

"STOP IT, MAMA, STOP IT! THIS IS CRAZY! YOU'RE HURTING YOURSELF—YOU'VE GOT TO STOP THIS!"

She looked up at my wild, distorted face and opened her mouth in a wordless whimper. I think she thought that I was going to hit her.

But I could not—did not want to stop; a lifetime of repressed rage and fear was pouring out of me.

"MOM—THERE'S NOTHING WRONG WITH YOUR SCALP! THERE'S NO DISEASE!! YOU'RE DEPRESSED, AND YOU NEED TO SEE A PSYCHIATRIST!"

In my frenzy I went on, saying the unsayable:

"Ever since I can remember, you've found some reason to pick at yourself! I'VE ALWAYS HATED THAT! I HATE YOU FOR IT!"

She remained stupefied, mouth open, staring up at me. But nothing indicated that she had comprehended a word of what I'd said.

Still rigid with anger, I turned and walked back to my bed, lay down on my side, shaking, legs drawn up to my chest.

"Oh, God, the poor thing. Poor, crazy little old thing."

I felt deep shame, guilt—and an enormous sense of relief.

"She had it coming! She's always had it coming!"

After a time, I heard her silent return to the bed. I lay there a long time, wondering what things would be like in the morning, and for the rest of our lives.

When I opened my eyes to pale morning light filtering through the leaf-patterned drapes, I was startled to see the door opening from the corridor. My mother, fully dressed and assembled with teeth, hearing aid and, no doubt, panty-girdle, was coming through the door holding two steaming paper cups of coffee.

"Oh, coffee! Great! Where'd you find it?"

"There's a snack bar on the mezzanine."

Her voice was calm, her face blank.   She put the cups on the round table and sat down cautiously in one of the padded chairs that surrounded it. I took a seat across from her and tried the insipid coffee.

"Mom, let's talk."

"About what?"

She opened a plastic thimble of half-and-half and poured it into her cup.

I was trembling, trying to keep my voice low and steady, yet loud enough for her to hear.

"Mom, I'm so sorry for yelling at you last night. I didn't want to hurt you, but I did want to scare you into doing something that actually treats your condition. I'm sure that you're clinically depressed. The right doctor could prescribe antidepressants that will make you feel so much better!"

She stirred a little stick around in her cup.

"You mean a psychiatrist."

"Yes. They know much more than most doctors about which mood-altering medicines are effective for things like this. Mama, I am really afraid for you!"

She set her chin in a very familiar, stubborn way.

"Well, don't be. I won't be around much longer. This disease is going to kill me before long."

I moaned softly and touched her hand, which still wore the

tiny silver-and-diamond engagement ring my father had given her some sixty-six years before.

"You're not going to die for a long time, Mom. We'll be back here again next year."

"I doubt it. Unless I can get this stuff off me. If I keep working at it, I might be able to get it all. But it's very hard! Nobody knows."

———

Footnote: Soon after that, I spoke to Lucy's GP in Florida, who prescribed an antidepressant "for her nerves." The obsession gradually disappeared, and she lived well into her ninety-fourth year.

By the Way, Ma..., 1977

Rachel, my darling daughter, who never feigns anything, put down her fork and, feigning nonchalance, said, "By the way, Ma, I think I'm gay."

I have no idea what we were talking about before that moment, so what her statement was "by the way" of, I'll never know.

Her brother Ben took another massive helping of lasagna from the casserole dish in the center of the round oak kitchen table.

I swallowed a mouthful of broccoli and looked skeptically at Rachel, home from the University for the weekend.

"Honey, are you sure? I mean, what makes you think so?"

"Mom, she'd hardly *say* so if she wasn't *sure!*" Ben's voice was turgid with fifteen-year-old contempt.

I kept my focus on my sweet girl, whose fair, glowing skin had never known nor required makeup, and whose hazel eyes were always lucid. When she was three, she had made up a verse that began,

"You know where I was;
my nature was so clear,
that all the horses and all the men
were died in the silverware."

(The end gets a bit off track, but still, I've always believed, she had correctly defined herself.)

In those long-ago days of my kids' babyhoods, I had written down every brilliant thing they said; some of their creations are still legible in their baby books, despite being hauled around from house to house in Blairstown, New Jersey, to Menlo Park, California, and finally now, to my small, beloved home in Santa Cruz.

Rachel's baby book also contained a fluff of her then white-blond hair, and a few black-and-white photos of her as a cute little bundle with one chubby leg in a cast (she'd been cramped in my womb, and was born with a turned, or "clubbed" food, which was splinted immediately after her birth.) Her nurses had signed their names and good wishes on the two-inch cast, which Rachel, kicking and cooing like any happy baby, never seemed to notice. That tiny, frayed plaster treasure, which had to be replaced twice as she grew out of them over the first six months of her life, had perfectly corrected the malleable bones. Wrapped in silk, the first and smallest of the casts still resides in my scarf drawer.

Now, a healthy university freshman with a headful of innumerable books, and a strong, slender body, she scraped the remains of her dinner to one side of her plate and looked up at me from under her eyelashes, flushing slightly.

"Well, I'm *pretty* sure. I mean, I haven't *done* anything—yet—not really—but ... you know I've never been attracted to boys, and I *am*, sometimes, to girls."

I felt myself retreat into my counselor persona—thoughtful,

nonjudgmental, searching for alternative causes for offbeat feelings and behavior. I pushed my chair back from the table.

"Well, honey, you've more or less lived in *books*; maybe you
haven't had enough life-experience yet. I think you're the kind
of girl that young men might not notice until, further along in
college, when they're sort of—*winnowed down*—to those with
more mature tastes, interested in a serious kind of woman.
That's what happened to me in grad school, guys were . . ."

Rachel's facial expression, which had gone from mildly
anxious to something between acute aggravation and major
eye-rolling boredom, made me stop myself in the midst of my
homily.

She spoke then with force and decisiveness: "Mom, I'm
going by my *own* feelings—not *theirs*! I just don't seem to have
any feelings for boys—not *that* kind!"

Ben, who had slid down in his chair until his long body was
about to end up on the floor, pulled himself into sitting
position.

"I think it's cool!" He scooted his chair closer to his sister,
who had in recent years, become considerably smaller than he.
He grabbed her shoulders and tried to noogie her head, hooting,
"*My sister, the Dyke!*"

She fended him off but grinned in his direction. He
stretched over the table to retrieve his half-filled plate and fork
and continued gorging his lasagna.

I can't say the possibility of Rachel being a Lesbian had
never crossed my mind. She tells me that when she first went
away to college, I called her often, asking about her classes, her
new friends, and whether she'd met any *nice boys*. A far as I
knew, she had never yet shown an erotic interest in either girls
or boys.

She looked, I thought, appealing, feminine: her dark-blond
hair was long, straight and silky, her figure with well-developed

young breasts, athletic and lithe. Like all her friends and most everyone else in those strange times, (the late sixties and seventies), she lived in jeans; but she liked granny-dresses, and had made herself some pretty ones.

She'd never dated in high school, never shown interest in going to proms and dances, finding her social life among the kids, mostly girls, with whom she went to grade school. But she'd never seemed to feel she was missing anything, wasn't depressed or sad, and I was confident that she had never gone through the kind of tortures that had plagued me from early childhood, hankering after one unattainable boy or another.

During the frantic years after my painful divorce from their father—Rachel was eight, Garth (Davy), six and Ben, four—I had gone to grad school to become a licensed clinical social worker at a county mental health center. As a full-time psychotherapist and single parent, I'd seldom taken time to ponder my daughter's social life: I was mostly just grateful for her apparently levelheaded immunity from adolescent angst.

We'd had a few quarrels, during her early teens, most of them based on my futile attempts to get her to be—well, just a little more *ordinary.*

"Yes, you do have to wear shoes to school, for heaven's sake, and brush your hair!" "Honey, wouldn't you like to get a shorter haircut, like they're starting to wear now?"

She had a loving relationship with her dad, an alternately ebullient and depressed sculptor, and spent time with him regularly, usually with her brothers. With his new wife, he had a house on the beach at *Ano Nuevo,* a perfect place for kids to spend happy days on the sand and in the tidepools near the shore.

So far, on this fateful evening, my training had allowed me to remain calm outside, the good counselor-- but internally,

I was crying out to my mentors, "So *what am I supposed to do now?*"

From my studies, and, even more so, from the painful stories of my gay clients, I knew some huge *no-nos* for a parent in this situation. In fact, I realized, I had already done one of them—my first words had discounted her declaration as a possible youthful phase, or a mistake.

But beyond all other considerations, I knew with complete confidence, that I would not jeopardize our relationship, the passionate connection I had felt for her from the moment I knew of her presence in my body.

I leaned close and took her hand. "Well, sweetie, gay or straight, whatever you are is completely fine with me, you know that."

"I know it, Mama." She lay her head on my shoulder, her face suffused with love and relief.

"I feel so lucky—some of my friends have lost their families —if they've even felt they could come out to them."

But the truth is, even as I basked in the warmth of her trust, I clung to the possibility that she didn't really *know* . . . maybe she was being influenced in that direction by new friends at her college in Santa Cruz, a town and a campus where the spirit of Haight-Ashbury was still alive in the scruffy clothes, long hair, wild music, drugs, and free-ranging sexual experimentation.

I had thought her immune to most of those temptations, which I believed had been in large part the cause of the collapse of my marriage—if not, for that matter, for the end of civilization as we knew it!

But she was *my daughter*, after all—how could she not, ultimately, be drawn to some sweet boy, with his beautiful new grownup body and his shadowy beard, tentatively cocky from past conquests—or more likely, vulnerable, hoping for a relationship with a nice girl as shy and inexperienced, as bookish—

perhaps as artistic—as he? How could she resist a man's *other-ness*—his puppy-like roughness and randy smells, his peculiar fascination with sports and engines, his openness to exploration and adventure? Of course, I realized, there were *women* with these qualities, too.

I have to admit that, for months after that fateful dinner, I nourished the foolish hope that Rachel would eventually take note of some adorable guy, find herself thinking about him whenever she heard a love song, and then, when he finally had the courage to approach her—or vice-versa—*normal* feelings would naturally develop.

My kindly internal (*Jungian*) therapist frequently reminded me that feelings of all kinds, including love and sexual attraction for one's own sex are perfectly normal, wholly worthy—in themselves; it is *acting* on such feelings that one must carefully consider. For, if Rachel did prove to be a Lesbian, what I most dreaded was that the world might never see her, my brilliant girl, as her unique, perfect self! She'd be one of society's oddballs, scorned by the so-called normal masses of human beings. I couldn't bear the thought of that.

I looked for causes. There was little talk of genetics in those days, almost every discrepancy in human behavior was attributed to upbringing (i.e., the mother.) Obviously, in *this* case, it would be the *father's* fault. If Stuart hadn't walked out on us when she was seven—the pinnacle of a little girls' romantic attachment to her father—smashing the foundations of her world—how could she trust a man, ever again?

Naturally, she would turn to women: in her experience, women stick around.

But then, said the therapist (*assuming the role of harsh real-ist, as my Gestalt trainers would have done*), Stuart didn't desert the *children*—just *you*. Rachel knows he has always loved her, and she loves him. If *you*'d had more self-esteem, had pulled yourself together without so many days when your little daughter, her tender heart wrenched with pity for her grieving mother, brought you tissues and lukewarm tea, sat beside you and stroked your bedraggled hair—the break-up and divorce wouldn't have been so traumatic for her! It's at least as much *your fault* if she's Queer!

And what's so great—my ruthless Gestalt guru would press her point with lofty, professional belligerence—*about heterosexuality? How many women and girls have you counseled who've been betrayed, deserted, beaten, raped or otherwise had their precious innocence violated by their male lovers, husbands, relatives? Your problem is, your father was a kind man, who loved your mother, despite her flaws, and stayed with her for a lifetime. You've been hunting for his equivalent all your life—and look what you've come up with! Doesn't it make a lot more sense for Rachel to team up with a woman—someone who's not driven by lust every waking moment, who doesn't have to prove how macho she is by winning at everything—sex, work, games? Don't knock Lesbianism, lady, until you've tried it!*

I tried to imagine myself making love with a woman. I knew several with whom I'd certainly be more compatible than any of the men I'd dated in the years since my divorce. I found women beautiful, cherished them as friends and companions. But the chemistry wasn't there. I was still drawn to men, the rough, smelly brutes—though I preferred those who bathed regularly.

And so I pondered, while fifty miles away, in a shining white, Mediterranean-style campus shaded by soaring redwood trees and overlooking the azure crescent of Monterey Bay, Rachel was dealing with her first experiences in love, with nothing to guide her except a library full of novels and history books. She had chosen to major in Womens' Studies, which I feared, would not be helpful, either in meeting a suitable man or in learning to place faith in that gender as a whole.

Whenever I called her, I'd tread as lightly as possible around personal questions. As always, she excelled in her academic work, and she volunteered that she'd gone to a college party.

"It was really fun, Mama, we danced outdoors in the Plaza circle—everybody took their shoes off and we danced in our stocking feet."

"No kidding! We used to call that a sock-hop, in the gym at school."

"It can be a problem, though—everybody leaves their shoes at the edge of the circle, but when I went back to get mine, I couldn't tell which ones were mine! There must've been, like, fifty pairs of identical brown Birkenstocks!"

"Well, I hope you picked some good ones—those things cost a fortune."

"I'm pretty sure I found my own. After that, I wrote my name in them."

"Honey," I ventured gently, "what about children?"

"Huh?"

"If you—go with women, sweetie—I'm so afraid that you'll miss out on the greatest happiness a woman can have in life— having a baby."

(And here my therapist self simply dissolved into a hysterical woman.)

I wailed, *"And what about my grandchildren?"*

There was a long silence, broken only by the muffled pandemonium of three or four stereos competing through the thin walls of her student dorm.

Then, ignoring my histrionics, she replied coolly, "At this point, Ma, I don't think I ever *want* to have children. Garth and Ben are bound to give you a bunch of grandbabies. But, if I do decide to have them, there are ways . . . Lesbians have kids all the time. I know this woman who used a turkey-baster . . ."

"*Oh, God.*" I took a deep breath and pulled myself together.

"Well, honey, you're coming home for Easter vacation next Friday, right? I'll pick you up at the bus station. . ."

"Okay, the six-fifteen.   And Mama, I'd like to bring a friend.   Her name's Alicia Rivera—Ally—you haven't met her yet.   I was hoping maybe she could stay with us a couple of days?"

The skin on the back of my neck began to prickle, and I had to force myself to breathe. "Sure, sweetie! . . . Is Ally—a friend from your dorm?"

"No, she's a junior, in Women's Studies—she's got a room downtown, the lucky duck!   She doesn't have to cope with dueling stereos day and night!"

Then her voice became soft, dreamy, a tone I'd never heard from her before.

"You'll like her, I know. She's a lot like you, she cares so much about people, about the world . . .We're lovers, Mama. And we're both strict vegetarians, so don't make us any ham or turkey or anything with a face."

"Oh, honey. . ."

So there it was. Deal with it. In the next few days I wrestled with the kinds of knotty questions most parents of nearly-grown children must face, sooner or later. Should I make up the sofa-bed in the living room, or just expect Ally to share Rachel's bed, as in the past when she had a friend for an overnight? What, then, if in a few years, one of the *boys* brought home a girlfriend—or, God forbid, a *boyfriend* for the night? My kids knew that I hadn't been a saint since their father left—how could I pull that "not while you're living under MY roof" routine?

I tried not to think about what the girls might actually do in bed. They were so young, maybe they just hugged and kissed? At most, I thought, they might engage in mutual masturbation, on the fine points of which I, a California Certified Sex Therapist, had encouraged and instructed sexually inhibited individuals and heterosexual couples.

Or would Ally, who was older and presumably more experienced, turn out to be a belligerent truck-driver type with a butch haircut, hiking boots, even—Oh my God—*tattoos!*—like a man in all respects, except for the unrestrained breasts under her plaid flannel shirt. In that case, she might arrive with a suitcase full of implements to substitute for her missing penis! Could my impressionable daughter, in the few weeks since I'd last seen her, have modeled herself after this hooligan, cut off her beautiful hair and learned how to swear and swagger? The more I thought about the weekend, the more anxious I became.

The Greyhound was late, as usual. I sat in my car in the bus station parking lot, deep breathing, and mumbled the mantra, which I had thought up for myself when I was a small child: Oh, dear, oh, dear, oh dear, oh dear!

At last, the blue-and-silver monster lumbered into the shelter of the station portico. I stepped out of my car and walked slowly toward the open front door of the bus, where the driver was giving an arm to an elderly man with a cane. Then there emerged the usual straggle of sedated-looking teenagers, women with crumpled sacks stuffed with god-knows-what, a young woman with a whining toddler.

Where were the girls? Had they missed the bus? Is it a variation on Murphy's Law that the person you're waiting for is always the last one out?

Finally, there she was, bouncing down the steps, my Rachel, her hair streaming down the back of her maroon sweater. She looked around, beaming and waving when she spotted me. Right behind her, there descended a small, plump

person, wearing round, gold-rimmed glasses, jeans and a flowered turtleneck. She had a cap of short, wavy brown hair and a
soft, pretty face, which dimpled as she smiled and took Rachel's
hand.

Rachel tugged the young woman towards me, and did not
let go of her hand when she ran into my arms, so that I found
myself, willy-nilly, hugging this new daughter of mine, as well:
this Ally, whose gentle sweetness and quick, thoughtful intelli-
gence would enrich our family for a long time to come.

Class Photos, 1949

Mrs. Butner posed like a Shakespeare tragedienne before our class of unusually well-groomed seniors. Her bare arms in the drab, short-sleeved rayon print dress reached out, as if to gather every tiny flicker of attention from her much-preoccupied audience of thirty students—the entire graduating class of Marlborough High School, 1949. Her watery amber eyes shone behind rimless glasses, her gestures more than usually animated and expressive.

It wasn't often that we all listened to Mrs. Butner—I tried to never listen to her screechy voice, and for most of my classmates, who knew her all too well from the required courses she had somehow attained a monopoly to teach, year after year—U.S. History, Missouri History, Government, and this senior class, Civics—tuning her out was second nature.

But today, she had an exciting story to tell, and her flair for drama lent her a kind of magnetism, as she walked back and forth in front of us, taking prissy little steps in her brown two-inch heels, mimicking a respectable (white) lady going about her business.

"So, class, there I was, downtown—in broad daylight--just coming out of Peck's, the nicest store in the city—at Tenth and Main, you know—and along comes this nigger woman and she just grabbed my purse off my arm and ran!"

She turned her head slowly from left to right, making sure we could all see her thin, lightly wrinkled, powdered and rouged face, portraying the horror she had felt at this unthinkable violation (whether of her person, the handbag, or the sacred-to-whites-only upscale department store sidewalk, wasn't entirely clear). A few students made small shocked sounds. In my back-row seat, I closed my eyes and tried to slide down under my desktop.

"Well, of course, I screamed, and I tried to chase after her —'course, like most nigger gals, she was a big, fat old thing and couldn't run fast—but me, wearing my town shoes, I tripped and almost fell down right there on the sidewalk! Thank heavens, some nice white man came along and grabbed my arm just in time!"

Danny Markle one of her favorites, raised his hand, but he knew he didn't have to wait for her to call on him.

"Did she get away?"

"Well, of course, she got away—do you think there was a policeman around when he was needed?"

Her eyes flashed with joyful indignation.

"But by then, a whole crowd of nice friendly people—white people, of course—gathered around me, kind as they could be! One lovely gentleman even paid for my taxi fare home . . . I didn't even have a nickel for the streetcar!"

Martha Hupp, the Baptist minister's daughter, raised her hand.

"Martha?" Mrs. Butner smiled at the girl's sympathetic expression.

"That must have been just awful! It's such a shame there's

such wicked people in the world! But, as you said, there are nice people, too, always ready to help someone in trouble."

The teacher patted her wiry, permed red hair, which had become disheveled during her vigorous performance.

"You are so right about that, Martha, honey! Not that you can expect anything else from niggers—they have no sense of right and wrong to speak of. But you don't expect to find them right in front of a nice downtown store like Peck's! Now, if I'd been in Niggertown, or close to the baseball stadium, I surely would not have had my purse right out in plain sight like that— not that I'd ever be caught dead in those kind of places!"

Hunched over my carved and stained desk, I knew my stomach might spew at any moment. I couldn't bear what was going on, though such edifying lessons weren't uncommon in this teacher's classroom. I'd tried, a time or two in class, to take her on, with no result except for lower grades on my report cards, and Danny and some of the other idiot kids calling me "nigger-lover!"

But today was Picture Day, when we seniors were having our formal portraits taken for the 1949 Yearbook, and everybody was dressed up, including me, in my pretty forest green crepe dress. And I was definitely going to throw up! The teacher saw my posture, the look on my pale face; she knew her enemy. She moved closer to my desk.

"So, Susy, what do you have to say about all this? Don't you agree that something's got to be done about these niggers?"

She had taken to calling me "Susy" several months back, after I played a role with that name in a school play. Whenever I corrected her, she'd say, "Well, honey, you just look so much like a Susy, I keep forgetting it's not your name!")

"It's Janice, ma'am. I'm going to throw up!"

"Oh, well, Su—Janice," she giggled—I guess you better run to the little girls' room!"

I was already out the door.

In the restroom, I vomited my breakfast into the toilet, flushed it, rinsed my mouth at the basin and then shut myself in the stall and sat and thought.

Year after year, this ignorant, vapid, venomous woman made almost no attempt to teach the subjects that young people —us—we—needed to know in order to be good citizens and thoughtful people—not to mention, competent parents. Instead, she used most of this crucial learning time to indoctrinate kids with the ideas and the language of hatred towards people with dark skin—Negroes, as they were then called.

For the most part, my classmates were working-class kids whose upbringing already inclined them to believe in the inferiority of anyone different from themselves; they accepted her rants with bored indifference. I didn't know about the many suffering hundreds of students who had come before us, but nobody in our class, except me, had ever told her she was wrong.

For me, in those extremely "un-woke" years, the whole matter of race was simple: there were black kittens and white kittens, all equally lovable. People were people. When I was small, my Granny, a teetotaling ex-schoolteacher from an Abolitionist family in Illinois, had told me terrible stories about little Black children whose lives were ruined by white hatred. Those stories had grieved me greatly and began forming a sense of justice that has stuck with me all these years.

I was aware that, although I had grown up feeling sympathy and interest in "colored people" (another acceptable term in those days), I'd never really known any of them! No Black people resided in the various parts of the city where my family had lived—and there were no desegregated schools anywhere, that I knew of. As a Girl Scout, I had met a few Negroes my own age at conferences in downtown Kansas City, where I admired the neatly uniformed, pigtailed girls who represented their own (segregated) troops.

Sometimes, I was hastily introduced to the women who came to clean floors and do the ironing at Aunt Vivian's house, but they were busy and had no time to get acquainted with a white kid.

My only other opportunity to see Negroes was on the long streetcar rides I often took from Marlborough to the public library in downtown Kansas City. The track ran through the middle of a long area, called "the Paseo," which, during World War II, became heavily populated by Negroes, who came north to work in the defense plants. They were bone-tired people who'd worked hard since early morning, now riding home on those crowded, noisy cars that were also enlivened by groups of boisterous Black teenagers. But in those days, no Black person would dream of sitting down by a white one of any age, no matter how crowded the car.

In my childhood, I had seldom seen any but black and white faces; no foreign languages were spoken in my small world. I'd read nearly every "classic" English language novel in my school library and was deep into the card-file of the Kansas City Library's Adult Fiction section. But our Marlborough High School, which was located just south of the city and operated under Jackson County authority, offered us no foreign languages! No wonder I longed for the foreign, the different, the exotic. I couldn't wait for the chance to go away to college —I'd be the first person in my family to do so. I ached to find a life that was not completely bland and homogenous; a place where people were educated, tolerant, refined.

But, meanwhile, I was leaving Marlborough High School forever in a few days, and I knew that, while I still had the chance, I must try to stop Mrs. Butner in her fouling of kids' minds and hearts.

I'd managed to quiet my offended stomach, smooth my hair and refresh my lipstick just in time to take my place in front of the photographer's tripod—although a smile was beyond me that morning.

Everybody was milling around in the combination gym/auditorium where a makeshift photography studio had been set up on the stage. The seniors stood in their usual small cliques, waiting to have their pictures taken, or for friends who were still nervously combing their hair or, in case of the boys, retying their ties in preparation for their big moment.

I slid in between my two best friends, sitting on a wooden bleacher.

"Have you been up there yet?"

Shirley answered, "I have, but MaryElla Westfall, here, is, as always, way down at the bottom of the alphabet!"

MaryElla pretended to pout. "Oh, girls, I'm so fretful, I'm sure that by the time I get up there, I'll not only have eaten off all my lipstick, but both of my luscious, sensationally kissable lips right along with it!"

She was the most recent addition to our class, having moved from Texas at the beginning of the school year. She was very smart, kind and funny, and I loved her right away.

I said, "It's not so bad—the photographer's kinda cute, and he makes you laugh. Anyway, you always take a great picture!"

"Well, how can one help it, sugar, when she's just naturally gorgeous?" She batted her huge, heavenly-blue eyes, tossing her thick brown hair.

"Hey, Janice, what happened to you in Civics this morning?" Shirley asked. "Were you really sick?"

"Yeah, I threw up. Butner did it to me again. I just can't stand the way she talks!"

I scooted as close as I could to the other girls, lowering my voice.

"Listen, I've decided that we've just got to do something about her! She's totally rotten! And remember, we all have younger brothers who'll eventually have to sit through her garbage for four years! What I think we should do: we'll all go to Superintendent Harrison's office and tell him exactly what she does—and doesn't do! He ought to know that she says 'nigger' all the time—and what a terrible teacher she is!"

Shirley, a honey-blonde, whose mother was president of the PTA, slid a few inches away from us.

"Oh, gosh, hon, why make trouble? We'll be out of here next week, and we'll never have to see her again—and my little brother's smart, he already knows she's an idiot."

"But a lot of kids don't know that! They'll listen to her and think she's right! Doesn't it make you sick to think of her going on this way, year after year? Shirley, your mom has always been active in school affairs, and everybody knows you—if you speak up it'll mean something!"

Shirley shook her head emphatically.

"Oh, sorry, Janice, I absolutely couldn't do that! My parents would have fits if they found out I was trying to get a teacher fired!"

Her gaze roamed around the gym, lighting on Carlton Banks, a dull but good-looking boy she sometimes dated.

"Hey, I'll see you guys later—I've gotta talk to Carlton about the prom." She grabbed her purse and headed across the basketball court toward a cluster of boys.

I sighed, looking trustfully into MaryElla's sweet face.

"Shirley's been my best friend since fifth grade, you know—but she never really cares about anything serious. Anyway, I'm counting on you to go to Mr. Harrison with me."

My friend hung her head for a moment, blushed and shook her head lightly, laying her pretty hand on mine.

"Janice, I'm so sorry—you know I'd love to help you out with anything, ordinarily—but I just can't see gettin' involved in this kind of sticky business right now. I just want to get out of here with my diploma and marry Tommy!"

Her eyes went dreamy as she spoke her fiance's name.

"You and Shirley are going to be in the wedding, of course —you're wearing purple satin gowns, with scoop necks and cap sleeves—and of course, I'll wear my Mama's lace wedding gown, with a bouquet of white and lavender flowers."

I briefly pictured myself in a purple satin gown, and then snapped back to the painful reality that my best friends, two of the most popular and smartest girls in school, had turned me down in my hour of need.

"I know, honey—I can't wait," I told MaryElla, ambiguously.

I stood up and looked around the gym.

"Maybe I can get Natalie and Martha to go with me."

"I surely do hope so, honey; you don't want to confront old Mr. Harrison by yourself! I don't believe I've ever seen him smile at a kid, let alone talk to one."

"I'll see you after school—I'm going to try to catch up with Nat."

I reached the girl just as she was heading out the door. Natalie was the tallest girl in class, and the most athletic. I knew she was on her way to her part-time job at the A&P.

"Hey, Nat, you have your picture taken already?" I hurried to match her long strides.

"Yeah, it'll be a beaut, like always. I'm sure I blinked just as he snapped the picture."

"Did you smile?"

"Sorta. He made me say cheezits. Anyway," she grinned

with a shrug, "I always look like a horse in photos."

I admitted to myself that the girl's long, broad face, surrounded by wheat-colored, whacked-off hair, was kind of horsy. But she had a kindly disposition and a straightforward honesty that made me like and trust her.

I said, "After Civics class this morning, my picture'll probably look like I have a fatal disease! I had to go throw up!"

"Oh, yeah, she makes me sick, too. I'm so glad I'm getting out of here. After graduation, I start in full-time at the store. I'm savin' up to buy a used car this summer. You want to go swimming out at Sather Lake sometime?"

She pushed open the heavy outside door.

"I'd love it! But, wait a sec, I want to ask you something."

"Okay, what's up?"

I lowered my voice.

"I'm going to Superintendent Harrison's office to tell him about Butner—the way she talks about Negroes and how she never even pretends to teach us anything about history or government? Somebody in authority ought to know what she's doing, year after year!"

Nat frowned and nodded. .

"Uh, yeah, okay—I guess so—she's really the pits. I'll go with you. When?"

"Great! I'll go ask his secretary for a good time to see him. And I'm going to get Martha and maybe a few others to go with us."

"Okay. See you tomorrow." She loped off down the street.

I went back inside and spotted Martha Hupp on a high bleacher, frowning at a problem in her geometry workbook. Her short blonde hair had been carefully curled under for the photo, and she wore a starched and ironed white blouse with a broomstick skirt she'd made in Home Ec.

I bounced up the bleachers and sat down beside her. "Hi,

Martha, you all through down there?"

"Yes, and I'm sure glad that's over! If I don't get this stuff done before I go home, the kids'll never let me study."

I knew that Martha had to babysit four younger siblings, while her parents were busy with church duties.

"I don't want to hold you up, but I just wanted to ask if you'd go with Natalie and me—and maybe some others—to talk to Superintendent Harrison about Mrs. Butner?"

The girl's light eyes widened and her cheeks flushed slightly.

"Wow, that's a wild idea! I never heard of any kids here complaining to the superintendent about a teacher before! But, shouldn't we go to Principal Jakes? I believe he's her immediate superior."

"There's no use in that, he's another redneck—he's almost as bad as Butner herself. I think Harrison is our only hope—I imagine that he must have got an actual college degree sometime in the ancient past."

"Well, you're very brave, Janice; but I'm not really sure it's the right thing to do." She looked solemnly into my eyes, and said, "I'll pray about it tonight, and let you know tomorrow."

"Thanks. I am sure it's the right thing, and I believe you will be, too."

As I stood up to go, she picked up her workbook with a sigh.

"See you tomorrow!"

I felt slightly more hopeful, as I hurried down the bleacher stairs and approached a group of guys, who, deprived by the picture-taking set-up of actual basketballs, were throwing imaginary lay-ups at a real basket.

As I stood watching and listening to their loud, crude jokes, I decided that asking them was fruitless, and moved on to a few other girls I hoped might be willing to join our small rebellion.

But each of them looked at me with amazement, suspicion and/or hostility, and made no bones about telling me they would have no part of such a crazy notion.

Carrie Campbell, whose parents ran a beer-joint down near the train tracks, looked like she wanted to slap me.

"Are you crazy? You really gonna stand up for those jiga-boos? Butner's right, the niggers are gettin' in every place. They'll be movin' out here one of these days, and then you'll see—wherever they go, they wreck the whole neighborhood!"

I knew there was no use trying to change made-up minds like Carrie's. I'd noticed that people often got a kind of lunatic gleam in their eyes and spoke with more passion about "the niggers" than even politics or football.

I straightened my shoulders (adults were always telling me to pull my shoulders back, "Stand up straight Janice!") and went into the superintendent's office to ask his secretary, Mrs. Wurtle, for an appointment.

The woman was surprised: students rarely came to see the superintendent, and when they did, it was to get permission for an activity involving all three levels—grade-school, junior high, and high school—since he had responsibility for all of them.

"Why sure, honey, he's got a few minutes before the lunch hour on Thursday—what's it about? Did you try Mr. Jakes?"

"No, ma'am." I tried to sound firm and decisive. "This is a particular situation that we think only Superintendent Harrison can deal with."

"Well, okay, I'll tell him you're coming." She frowned and blinked somewhat disapprovingly, mostly, I thought, because I'd given her no clue to what my business was with her boss. But then she smiled brightly at me.

"Of course, Janice—you're going to be valedictorian, aren't you? Such a bright girl, you've had nothing but A's ever since you started school!"

"No, ma'am, I'm pretty sure Martha Hupp is going to get it this year. I'm probably getting a C in Civics." (More likely an F after Thursday, I thought.)

"Oh, dear! That's a shame . . . but I just know you'll do very well, whatever path you choose after graduation."

I'd long ago given up caring about being valedictorian, even though it was humiliating, in such a tiny class. I'd made A's in Butner's classes the first two years, but for the past two, I'd been unable to make the effort to seem interested in her "lectures," and my grades showed it.

During the two days that followed, I had so much work to do that I didn't have time to get nervous about it—or to seek out other brave volunteers. There were finals, of course, and I was editor of the yearbook, which had to be ready to print as soon as the class pictures were back; I was on the decorating committee for the prom, and I had to rehearse my vocal solo for the Baccalaureate program. In such a tiny school, a few people do everything.

On Thursday morning, before class, I sought out Martha, who affirmed that she had prayed over the issue, as promised, and had been "called" to undertake this "mission." She and Natalie, whose persistent acne had flared up, as it did when she was nervous, agreed to meet me outside the superintendent's office at 11:30.

When we entered Ms. Wurtle's small outer office, she told us to go right in. I opened the door with its frosted-glass window upon which was inscribed, "Superintendent E. Edgar Harrison." We entered in a close gaggle, the other girls slightly behind me, and faced a large, well-upholstered man with thick gray hair and a broad nose on a pink, clean-shaven face, seated behind a large oak desk. There was only one chair for guests, and he did not suggest bringing in more chairs—so we stood.

The (to us) powerful man looked at us benignly, but

without a hint of interest in what our business with him might be. He patted a pile of neatly-stacked papers on his desk.

"Hello, girls—as you see, I'm very busy—I guess we all are at this time of year. But I try to make time for students when I can."

"Thank you for seeing us, Mr. uh, Superintendent Harrison," I said nervously, and plunged right in.

"We think there's a big problem in our school, and we knew you would want to know about it."

He nodded solemnly and said he was glad we had decided to bring our problem to him. He opened his arms and looked benignly at us from under heavy grey eyebrows.

"That's what I'm here for!"

I rushed on. "Well, the problem is Mrs. Butner. She is a really terrible teacher—we've all had her for the past four years —as you know, everybody has to take her courses to graduate— but, the truth is, she never really teaches us anything! She stands up there and—and chats, tells stories about her family and all kinds of irrelevant stuff—but we don't learn anything about history or government!"

Mr. Harrison's face reflected mild surprise, and amusement.

"Oh, come now, Janice! You mean you learned nothing at all? That hardly seems likely; Mrs. Butner has been a respected member of our little faculty for nearly ten years—you must have learned something from her along the way!"

"No sir, it's TRUE!" I gripped the edge of the desk, trying to convey the veracity and strength of my feelings. "Nobody in our class respects her—sometimes when she says something really trashy, the boys—well, most of us—just reach up and pull the handle on the—well, you know what I mean, we just flush her down!"

The man looked at me in astonishment for a few seconds,

then laughed with teacherly merriment. Then, resuming his most august demeanor, he turned his attention to my friends, still half-hidden behind me.

"You girls think Mrs. Butner is a terrible teacher?"

Natalie, her face rosy with acne and embarrassment, nodded, but Martha just stood there, trembling against my shoulder, and said nothing.

I stood as straight as possible, "shoulders back," and added the final straw, as I thought, to the case against our unbelievably harmful teacher:

"The worst thing, as far as we're concerned, is that she's always talking to the class about Negroes in a very hateful way. She calls them "niggers," and tells us stories about how they steal or smell bad, or, as she says, 'ruin the city.' It literally makes us sick!" I clasped my hands, almost pleading with the man. "You have to do something to stop her!"

He ignored that and beckoned Natalie and Martha to step forward.

"Now, I want you girls to tell me, do you feel that way, too, or is it just Janice that has these opinions?"

I turned desperately to each of them, but they moved further back and kept silent.

Then he focused back on me, and said, "I notice you're not making the good grades in her class that you used to, Janice. I can see why you might not like this particular teacher."

He picked up a small sheaf of loose papers and began squaring it up by bumping it on his desk. Then he looked straight at me with a clear, open, almost playful expression.

"So Mrs. Butner tells you stories about the darkies—what's wrong with that?"

I opened my mouth, but in my shock and disbelief at what I was hearing, no words came out. I realized that none were possible. In his own way this authoritative, somewhat educated man had expressed the same hateful, crude and deliberate igno-rance that I had heard all my life from people of much lower status.

Natalie opened the door, and we bumped through it in a convoluted huddle. Once outside on the school steps, Natalie said she had to get to work, and took off. Martha put her hand on my arm for an instant and said, "I'm sorry, Janice. . . I didn't know what to say."

"Me either," I said. "I didn't know what to say, either."

The '49ers Yearbook came out the last day before gradua-tion. My picture was actually lovely, with a serious but warm expression in my eyes, and all the flaws of complexion and consternation removed by the photographer's art.

It didn't look like me at all.

———

(Note to kids: Forget black kittens and white kittens—it's really *not* the same thing.)

This true story took place a half-dozen years before school integration, the Civil Rights Movement, and following that, the Black Power movement. They brought growing awareness in the country of the enormous complexities of racial problems, including ambivalence among Blacks about integration versus Black Nationalism. The deep and often justified distrust that many Blacks hold of well-meaning whites has, shamefully, held me back from active participation in antiracial efforts. Though I have had a few dear Black friends, I'm appalled at times by elements of racism that I still discover inside myself from my childhood—and, like most of us, I must continually struggle to avoid infection from the pervading national prejudice that still twists our minds and hearts.

The Green Beach, 1986

I wasn't old yet, just fifty-five, but I'd begun preparing for my own death when my Dad died of a stroke, a few years before. I'd made a will, put my house in a deed of trust for my kids, and signed a "do not resuscitate" document, copies of which resided with my daughter and two sons, and in my medical chart at the HMO. I knew very well that unexpected calamities can strike any time; also, I am of a philosophical turn of mind, and tend slightly toward depression.

But it had never occurred to me that my final moments of life would come this way; I've never achieved more than a clumsy dog paddle, so I usually keep out of deep water. I never imagined that I would drown!

I was on the fifth day of my first trip to Hawaii, a Sierra Club excursion, which, I was warned, would involve hard hiking, so for the past three months I'd amazed myself and my family by getting up every morning early to take a mile-run around my quiet Menlo Park neighborhood before work. By early August, when my annual vacation from a County mental health clinic came around, my legs and lungs felt much stronger than before.

For anybody who thinks Oahu is all luxury hotels on white beaches with palm trees and gentle surf and snorkeling, we hardy Sierra Clubbers know better. We were taken by bus to the far northeastern part of the island, where we were often rained on: our first night, we had a cold wind-and-rain-storm: our oldest camper, Eloise Cohen, age seventy-two, wiggled out of her pup tent just in time before it went tumbling end over end, down a grassy slope. We were obliged to huddle together in an open park shelter for the rest of the night. But we had sturdy, genial leaders, Bill and Harriet Weiss, schoolteachers who spent every summer leading these trips. They cooked wonderful meals for us on primitive equipment, and kindly encouraged anyone who seemed to be having a hard time.

On this glistening morning, after four days of hard but rewarding plods through lush tropical forests to coffee plantations and breath-taking waterfalls, the group of eleven women and five men, all dressed in hiking boots, shorts and long-sleeved shirts against the fierce tropical sun, had eaten breakfast early and headed out for a five-mile trek to the "Green Beach," where jade and other stones had worn away under the sea for centuries, to make a variegated greenish sand. We followed our guide, cook and mommy figure, Harriet, through exotic foliage, across charcoal-black, bubbling, steaming lava fields, dusty roads and pasture-land (maneuvering carefully around an aggravated black bull).

When we finally arrived, everybody collapsed, exhausted and perilously overheated, onto the sand of a small beach (which, to tell the truth, wasn't even all that green). But we were the only visitors at the time, and the beach was tucked into a pretty little cove with a rocky cliff at one end. Harriet had warned us beforehand that we couldn't swim there, and

sure enough, there was a posted warning: NO SWIMMING—
POWERFUL UNDERTOW!

After prying their sweaty feet out of thick socks and hiking
boots, most folks unwrapped and chowed down on our hearty
sack lunches, but I was still too hot to eat, while there, just a
few sandy steps away, was the Pacific Ocean, beckoning with
cool, placid wavelets— comporting itself, for all I could see,
much like the gentle surfs I knew in California. A few from our
group had ventured a few steps into that pale green coolness,
and it seemed to me that I might safely go in, just up to my
knees, holding tight to the thin, rocky ledges that protruded
around the base of the cliff.

Ahh, this was Heaven! I took a few cautious steps into the
water, gripping the rough stones with both hands. I wasn't able
to get a good grip on them, but I was not at all fearful— just
happy—oh, yeah!—when suddenly a powerful wave grabbed
me, pulled me down into its much colder depths as casually as
if I were a drift of sea foam—and after a few endless seconds,
tossed me up to the surface again.

When I was able to shake the streaming water out of my
eyes and take a gasping breath, I saw to my horror that I was at
least thirty yards out from the beach, where my companions
stood watching me, mouths open and screaming, as I flailed in
deep water, with no chance whatever to save myself.

Though I'm usually a sociable person, I'd been acting the
loner on this trip, wanting to rest from a stressful job. For eigh-
teen years I had listened to peoples' sad and tragic stories for at
least eight hours every weekday. I loved my work, feeling that
clients almost always felt better after talking to me. But for the
past couple of years, I'd also had to cope with a misogynistic
boss who provided no support for his beleaguered staff and
spent most of his work week with his feet on his desk. I have no
idea what he was thinking about—a comfy retirement, probably

—because I was too busy juggling a heavy caseload to ask him. Since my recent divorce—my second—and my kids grown up and gone—my life was my job, with little time or energy for anything else. I was often on call at night, after my day's work, which sometimes took more than ten hours, because the paper-work—all those case-notes—had to get done.

California's County Mental Health system had opened in the early seventies, well-financed from federal, state and county funds. The clinics were designed to substitute for many California State mental hospitals which were being closed, on the grounds that, except for sequestering people who were wildly deranged, they often did more harm than good. They tended to produce people who got little therapy except for medicine, and often became "institutionalized," that is, so dependent on the hospitals' 24/7 support, however dreary and meager, that even if their mental conditions were much improved, they could not manage outside in the world.

The County clinics were open to all and hired well-trained and caring professionals—psychiatric social workers like me, psychologists and psychiatrists—to staff them. Our first duty was to help former mental hospital patients, newly forced out into so-called "halfway houses," where they would live in supervised small groups, and receive therapy and medication from the county clinics. But the much broader concept was also meant to offer low-cost psychotherapy to anyone who walked in the door, making it possible for many with emotional or mental illness to have their own shrink at minimal cost. A Socialist at heart, I was delighted to participate in this generous arrangement in its beginnings.

For many years, I had relished my work, knew I was good at it, was respected by my colleagues and usually appreciated by my clients. The job gave me scope to devise new techniques and ideas and put them into practice. I led dozens of innovative therapy groups, which not only allowed more folks to be treated in the hours available, but gave them new perspectives on other peoples' troubles, feelings, anger and compassion, while they learned to deal with their own knotty relationship problems.

But as the money was gradually withdrawn from the program over the years—and new, higher levels of hierarchy arose, with a much less compassionate perspective—the amount of energy for helping people had gradually given way to demands for mountains of repetitive paperwork under the heading of "accountability." And, sadly, our clientele had become limited to the chronically mentally ill.

In short, I was quite ready to leave, and would have been gone—except that I was getting older, with only the promise of a county pension after twenty-five years; and I needed ten years more. How could I, at fifty-five, leave the main source of support for my goddam golden years? Fifty-five, I knew, wasn't an ideal age to look for a new job.

"You can make it for ten more years," I told myself, gently but firmly. (I take the concept of my inner child seriously, and always try to talk to mine with compassion and affection.)

"You've been to enough serenity workshops. Just breathe deeply into your belly, practice positive thinking, self-hypnosis, yoga, tai-chi. You'll make it. *You are OK, sweetie!*"

But it was becoming harder to go there every day. I'd even considered asking one of my psychiatrist colleagues to give me a trial of Prozac.

———

Now, as the heedless ocean gulped me down and spat me up to the surface again, my arms flailing against the might of the jade-green water, my chief feeling was amazement at my plight. But, strange to say, I felt totally calm and accepting.

"I'm going to die now," I told myself, "and there's not a single thing I can do about it." It was a relief, really.

My life didn't flash before my eyes, but at some level, I instantaneously reviewed its accomplishments. I'd raised the kids, got them launched successfully into the world; loved my work until the system got too top-heavy; always treated people with caring and concern. I'd been madly in love twice and had more than my share of excellent sex. I'd traveled to Italy, England, Australia and Fiji. Once, at a secretarial job in New York City, I had actually met and shaken hands with my life-long idol, Eleanor Roosevelt!

"It's okay," I murmured to my cooperative inner child, "We're ready to go."

But the sea, in its cynical jocularity, wasn't through playing with me yet. In one long swoosh of its powerful tail, it shot me clear to the very edge of the shore. I scrabbled madly with both arms and legs to gain a foothold in the sliding, disintegrating soup of sand and pebbles, but there was no time—the wave flung me back again, leaving me even farther out!

At this point, finally, I got mad: shaking the sopping mat of hair out of my eyes, snorting and spitting the briny water, I yelled, *"Goddammit, NO! You're not gonna get me that easy!"*

I struck out with all my puny strength, and swam, gaining a yard or two before the next breaker plunged me deep into the blinding water, then up toward the beach once again, where the terrified on-lookers were screaming, urging me to *swim, swim!* This time, as I was thrown up to the beach on my belly, I dimly made out the outstretched arms of two women—dauntless Harriet and one other woman whose face I couldn't see. They each grabbed my wrists with both hands and hung on!

"Stand up!" They yelled. *"Get your feet under you, stand up, dammit!"*

But when I tried to plant my feet, the sea tugged me back,

my flopping legs as useless as the tail of a mermaid on dry land. The wave was pulling the other women down with me into the rolling quicksand under our feet. Close to exhaustion, but amazed at the fury with which my would-be rescuers demanded that I *stand the hell UP!,* I tried again and again to gain purchase—knowing that these amazingly brave women would soon have to let go or be drawn under themselves. And, at the last possible instant, my feet found something solid, my legs stiffened and steadied, and the two heroic women pulled me out of the surf and up onto the blessed dry sand!

I collapsed on the dry ground, stinging eyes squeezed tight shut, while the whole group— including several able-bodied men who had stood by gawking during the whole drama— gathered around me and my rescuers, all talking and yelling at once. I vaguely heard bits of Mrs. Cohen telling the story of the time she'd nearly drowned in the Plunge at Great Neck.

Harriet, still panting from her efforts, knelt beside me, to check whether I'd swallowed too much seawater, or was otherwise injured.

"I'm okay," I gasped out. "Thank you!"

Her voice was matter-of-fact, even terse.

"Sure, Jan, no problem. Don't even think about it."

All in a day's work, I guessed.

As soon as I could sit up and look around, I tried to figure out which of the other women had been my second savior, but by then, everybody was getting ready to leave, stuffing their gear into backpacks—and I couldn't tell. I remembered a tall, youngish body—but that could have been Lydia, the athletic librarian, or Rita, the corporate headhunter, or ... ? I didn't like to ask—what kind of idiot gets saved from certain death and doesn't even know who to thank? I felt mortified by my idiocy at going into the water when I'd been clearly warned not to. I had nearly killed myself and two others. I'd be surprised if any of the party ever spoke to me again. I couldn't even consider trying to comfort my inner child; right now, I had no patience for that clueless delinquent!

During the long, very hot march back to our campsite, my body chafed at every step by tiny, sharp grains of sand—a few of them green, perhaps—lodged in my bra and panties. Salt made a crust on my arms and legs. 1 was exhausted; but I plodded on, just grateful that the others didn't have to carry me—or my dead body. People walked beside me for short stretches, telling me how scared they were when I was out there, how glad I hadn't drowned.

Now it occurs to me that at least some of them were packing a load of guilt, for not coming to help the two struggling heroines—but at the time, I was too ashamed of myself to think of it.

A hot shower at the campsite, clean clothes, dinner—where to my relief, my adventure was already old news, scarcely mentioned. Finally, I escaped to my tent to wallow in my unworthiness, my humiliation—a heedless dork who should have known better! I didn't even light my lantern, just crawled into my sleeping bag, curled into a gut-comforting fetal position, sure that I'd lie awake all night berating myself.

The next thing I knew, the morning sun was glowing bright tangerine through the walls of my tent. I felt completely rested, and deliciously comfortable, with a new sensation, a sort of inflation under my ribs, and up into my shoulders and jaws—I couldn't quite place it.

I yawned, sat up, stretched, aware of a minor prickling of the tender skin in the crevices between my inner thighs and crotch where the sand had rubbed—and then I remembered: *I nearly died yesterday!* But t*oday—wow!* I was alive, and my life was very, very beautiful and infinitely precious! *That's* what that mysterious feeling was—*elation!*

I thought of my two saviors and felt proud and happy for them, too. Then I remembered our itinerary for the next two days, before flying home: we were to drive south and west to one of those gorgeous palmy beaches, lie on striped beach chairs under big umbrellas, like proper tourists, and—if I ever dared to enter the ocean again—to snorkel on a coral reef swarming with brilliant sea creatures.

As I brushed out my tangled hair, I thought about going back to work the next week, and was suddenly struck with the cliched, but spectacular realization: LIFE IS WAY THE HELL TOO SHORT!

I'll write my resume on the plane, I decided. With my experience and skills, my record of hard work and reliability, plus—I grinned to myself—my native *charm*—somebody's absolutely going to hire me!

A pleasant little breeze filtered through the tiny, screened porthole above my head. I smelled breakfast cooking—ham and French toast, if I wasn't much mistaken. I unzipped the tent and wriggled out of the tiny door—newborn!

Appendix: The Raging Granny Songs

I became a (self)-published author at age eighty, with the launch of my first novel, a somewhat-cozy mystery, *Dangerous Women*, followed two years later by a sequel, *An Un-Conventional Murder*. Both have protagonists who are—surprise!—old women in Santa Cruz, who work ferociously at their full-time volunteer jobs as members of the venerable (108-year-old) Women's International League for Peace and Freedom, begun by Jane Addams pre-World War I, in an attempt to prevent that horrible war.

Along with hard-working committees that focus on anti-nuclear, environmental, and anti-violence in all forms, our branch joined a growing number of WILPF groups in the U.S.

and Canada in forming a Raging Grannies gaggle: marching and demonstrating singers wearing old-timey dresses and hats, who, more or less musically, belted out our fury at the political messes into which our beloved country continues to sink more deeply with every passing year. We sang timely new lyrics to well-known old tunes and always invited our audiences to join in the singing. Although our gaggle, as this species is called, is now mostly in retirement, many Granny gaggles are still going strong in cities and towns around the world.

As a life-long scribbler of humorous verses, I became the main lyricist for the Santa Cruz Raging Grannies, publishing several songbooks over five administrations, with more than 200 songs of protest or support.

For anyone who likes political satire, the following examples—only a handful of the local, national and international issues we sing about—may provide a sense of the rage, the fun, and the powerful catharses that singing these songs gave us when we'd done everything else we could think of to draw people's attention to peace and away from violence. The following are mostly a bit moldy nowadays, but some are still crucially relevant. Some were written and sung, with fervor, during the past administration of a previous president who is hell-bent to command us again in November 2024.

For example, here's a song from the 1992 presidential campaign (only the names need replacing to serve again for 2024):

THE LUNATIC FRINGE ON TOP
(to the tune of "The Surrey With The Fringe On Top"*)

Intro:
The Right has set a novel precedent
They're sending in the clowns for president

We shake our heads and ponder what the hell they're
thinking—
Wonder where that Grand Old Party went?

Chorus:
Cain and Bachman, Romney and Perry
up there on the stage makin' merry—
We think things have got very scary
With the lunatic fringe on top!

Each candidate is more nuts than the last one
Each of 'em hopes they can pull off a fast one
If there's a winner, we sure can't forecast one
With the lunatic fringe on top!

The moderate right is so depressed
The radicals are front and center
Democracy in action at its madcap best—
A race any wacko can enter!

They want our votes, but I have to decline mine
These folks are all like a race out of Heinlein
They make Bush look like young Albert Einstein—
A demented crop!

They're the runt of the litter
They're the dregs of the coffee
They're the bats in the belfry
They're the lunatic fringe . . . . .On the top!

*Rogers and Hammerstein (OKLAHOMA), 1943

———

BRING 'EM HOME
(to the tune of "Country Roads")

Bring 'em home, bring 'em home
Bring them back where they belong...
They're our children—stop the killin'
Bring 'em home, bring 'em home.

They have gone off to learn how to kill and be killed—
Will they know how to love us,
and be kind? And be kind?

Those who made this evil war sent them off filled with lies
Some are cryin', some are dyin'
Broken hearts are their prize.

Are their hearts full of fear, are their souls filled with shame?
For their country they have slaughtered
Will they know whom to blame?

Bring 'em home, bring 'em home
Bring them back where they belong...
They're our children—stop the killin'
Bring 'em home, bring 'em home.

*James Taylor, 1971

WE'RE SITTIN' ON TOP OF THE BOMB
(to the tune of "Sittin' On Top of the World"*)

Oh, yeah, we're sittin' on top of The Bomb
Just holdin' our breath
We're frightened to death.
We're hopin' he won't start a war
by sending a text,
someday when he's vexed.

Nations quake and quiver
while madmen compete;
When will he deliver
His ultimate Tweet?

We're sittin' on top of The Bomb
Pretending we're cool,
like shooters at school.
Congress could lock up his toys
But they're so afraid,
Like scared little boys.

Madness is political
It starts at the top..
Nuke control is critical
Any day he might pop!
Yes, friends, we're sittin' on top of The Bomb
While craziness reigns we're wrackin' our brains!
The kids have shown us the way!
Get out and protest!
Get started today!

* Al Jolson, 1926

TEACHER'S PACKIN' A GUN
(to the tune of "Sunny Side of the Street"*)

Grab your lunchbox and your books
Don't forget that big red apple
Hope your homework's done—
cause your teacher's packin' a gun.

Don't you dare speak out of turn,
throw spitballs or erasers
school's no place for fun,
now that teacher's packin' a gun.

Now we should thank the PTA
they joined the NRA
sold cupcakes just to pay
for firearms
for school marms.

You'll be so much safer now
Miss Jones is locked and loaded
Your learning has begun
Cause your teacher's packin' a gun!

*Willie Nelson, 1978

———

SANTA CRUZ WEIRD
(to the tune of "California, Here I Come!"*)

Santa Cruz, you're very strange
Pray that this may never change.

Your writers, your artists, your politics
Are far from—the norm, but
nothing maryjane can't fix, cause
Down Pacific Avenue,
No one censors what we do—
The Grateful Dead are still revered—
Santa Cruz, you're truly weird!

Santa Cruz, you're looney-tunes
Ya got more swamis than saloons.
Your homeless are happy—now they can sleep!
The parks aren't so cozy, but spacious, and the rent is cheap.
So come on down and make the scene—
Every day is Halloween.
We're all befuddled, whack and cheered—
Santa Cruz, you're truly WEIRD!

That's why we love you—
Santa Cruz, you're truly WEIRD!

*Al Jolson, 1924

TORN AWAY
(to the tune of "Dixieland"*)

Oh, they left their homelands, like so many before them
Fleeing death by gangs or war,
they're torn away, torn away, torn away from their lands.

The helpless beg us just to be admitted
Jailed for "crimes" our own committed--

We were ALL refugees
Torn away from our lands

And the precious little children,
Oh hear their grief—
are thrown in filthy cages, crying out in fear and terror
Away, Away, they're torn away from Mami!
Away, Away, they're torn away from Papi!

As "zero-tolerance" is now our creed,
we punish those with utmost need—
Cast them away! Away! Far away from our door!

Our would-be fuhrer thinks he's one bad-ass
whose bigotry shows strength and class;
Put him away! Far away! We won't take any more!

And the precious little children, we all insist,
Must reunite with parents, who are sick with fear and sorrow—
Away! Away!
Away with ICE and tyrants.
Away! Away! Away with ICE and tyrants!

*Daniel Decatur Emmett, 1859

———

WE'RE LEGAL!
(To the tune of "Tea for Two"*)

Here am I, upon your knee
We're just plain folks, we're family
We're married as two souls can be—

We're LEEEEE-GAL!

No more petitions, no queer demonstrations,
We're almost accepted by distant relations
We're just Mom and Mom, it's a great situation—
We're LEEEE-GAL!

So now that our problems with marriage are mastered
Our sweet little child can't be labeled a bastard
Of course, we have in-laws, and that's a disaster, but
We're LEEEE-GAL!

When we're old and our limbs aren't so supple
We'll be bored to death like any old couple—

But we'll be together,
AND THAT'S WHAT IT'S ALL ABOUT!

*composer: Vincent Youmans; lyrics: Irving Caesar, 1924

———

HOLIDAY SONGS

GENERIC CAROL
(to the tune of "Deck the Halls")

Who's that baby in the cradle? Fa la la la la, la la la la
Give the babe a brand new dreidel, Fa la la la la, la la la la
We are celebrating Kwanzaa, Fal la la la la, la la la la
In the mobile park, De Anza, Fal la la la la, la la la la
Solstice is a new beginning, Fa la la la la, la la la la
Keep us free from sex and sinning, Fa la la la la, la la la la

Face the east and light a menorah, Fa la la la la, la la la la
Chant your mantra, dance your hora, Fa la la la la, la la la la!
Mother Mary's watching o'er us
Fa la la la la, la la la la

Singing a generic chorus
Fa la la la la, la la la la

While the Christians make a to-do, Fa la la la la, la la la la
Way down south we practice Voodoo, Fa la la la la, la la la la.
Let us now be realistic, Fa la la la la, la la la la
Some of us are atheistic, Fa la la la la, la la la la
While the faithful make devotions, Fa la la la la, la la la la
We're just going through the motions, Fa la la la la, la la la la!
Still and all, there is a reason, Fa la la la la, la la la la
Why we love this frantic season, Fa la la la la, la la la la
We just love to get together, Fa la la la la, la la la la
To warm our hearts in wintry weather,

Fa la la la la, la la la la!

―――――

CAPITALISTIC WONDERLAND
(To the tune of "Winter Wonderland"*)

Jingles sell, are you list'nin'?
At the mall, lights are glist'nin'
Just what hath God wrought?
It's something you bought
In our capitalistic wonderland.

All about, folks are shoppin'

Till our tote bags are poppin'
We don't have enough, so we're buyin' more stuff
In our capitalistic wonderland.

In Bloomies and in Macy's we have credit
That's good 'cause we lost our jobs in May.
When the bills arrive we will regret it,
But we are goin' shoppin' anyway.

We are knee deep in roses
Though we're up to our noses
In debts and in bills and all kinds of pills
In our capitalistic wonderland.

We used to have a realistic budget
Now we have to finance banks and wars
So we shrug our shoulders and say, "fudge it!"
We might as well just drive down to the stores!

As it sayeth in Deuteronomy,
"Thou shalt boost the economy!"
We're all good consumers in warm winter bloomers
In our capitalistic wonderland.
In our capitalistic wonderland!

*composer: Felix Bernard; lyrics: Richard Bernhard
Smith, 1934

All tunes can be found under their original title on YouTube.

Acknowledgements and Thanks

Thanks to anyone who finds, or suspects that they've found themselves in these stories. (I did try to warn you!)

My deep love and thanks to my dad, Francis Horne, for bolstering my entire life with his sturdy love, honesty, reasonableness, courage and hard work—and above all, his love of music, sense of humor, and having fun whenever possible!

I was blessed with the aid of my two collaborators: Sue Trowbridge, whose brilliant skills and energy actually brought the book to light; and earlier in the bewildering process of putting together the scraps of this crazy-quilt of stories, the author, editor and publisher, Debbra Palmer.

Special thanks to writer/police psychologist Ellen Kirschman and her husband, Steve Hollis Johnson, a builder and creative photographer, for their interest, time and help in making this book happen.

I could not have done any of this without my teacher Ellen Bass, the brilliant poet and co-author of a crucial contribution to the literature of women's emotional health, *The Courage to Heal*. She showed me that I could write.

Every day, I thank my great good fortune in my friend and helper, Evangelina Griego, who listens to my stories and keeps me going.

And to my beloved children, Rachel, Garth and Ben. You have continued to treat me with honesty, respect and hands-on help well into my dotage. You are my rock!

Made in the USA
Middletown, DE
24 February 2024

49812403R00099